The Smart Woman's Guide to Networking

By
Betsy Sheldon and Joyce Hadley

CAREER PRESS
3 Tice Road
P.O. Box 687
Franklin Lakes, NJ 07417
1-800-CAREER-1
201-848-0310 (NJ and outside U.S.)
FAX: 201-848-1727

THE SMART WOMAN'S GUIDE TO NETWORKING
ISBN 1-56414-207-8, $12.99
Cover design by Dean Johnson Design, Inc.
Printed in the U.S.A. by Book-mart Press

To order this title by mail, please include price as noted above, $2.50 handling per order, and $1.00 for each book ordered. Send to: Career Press, Inc., 3 Tice Road, P.O. Box 687, Franklin Lakes, NJ 07417.

Or call toll-free 1-800-CAREER-1 (NJ and Canada: 201-848-0310) to order using VISA or MasterCard, or for further information on books from Career Press.

Library of Congress Cataloging-in-Publication Data

Sheldon, Betsy.
    The smart woman's guide to networking / by Betsy Sheldon and Joyce Hadley.
        p.   cm.
    Includes index.
    ISBN 1-56414-207-8 (paper)
    1. Vocational guidance for women. 2. Women--Social networks.
3. Information networks. 4. Success in business. 5. Career development.   I. Hadley, Joyce. II. Title.
HF5382.6.S48 1995
650.1'3'082--dc20
                                                      95-36901
                                                      CIP

Acknowledgments

We are grateful for all those women and men who've contributed their expertise and experiences and shared their contacts so that this book could be written. They have become valuable members of our networks.

To Angelina Beitia, Lori Bennett, Sandra Borrer-Jury, Andra Brack, Betsy Brill, M. Kathryn Dailey, Evelyn English, Elena Gaoiran, Laura Gates, Melissa Giovagnoli, Sue Gould, Kim Hackett, Susan Hailey, Marilyn Johnson-Kondwani, Amy Jussell and Nancy Kingscott.

To Tomoko Lipp, Pamela Mills, Gretchen Minney, Ivan R. Misner, Lollie Moyer, Alice Ostrower, Angie Parker, Polly Pattison, Ginny Reed, Susan Shaner, Sandy Sohcot, Lya Sorano, Melissa Wahl, Thérèse Watley and Donna Wotton.

To Melanie Hadley, Lori Hitchcock, Joe Hnilo, Stacy McMullen, Jeanne Maillet and Barbara Oertli.

And a special thanks to Anne Robinson, whose critical eye and deft editorial touch we couldn't have done without.

Contents

Part 4: Networking to build your business

Introduction

It's happened to everybody.

You have your eye on a plum job. You think you're doing everything right: Working overtime to research the prospective employer, custom-tailoring your resume to address the employer's particular needs and meticulously polishing your interviewing style. Then one day, while you have your nose to the computer keyboard, somebody who "knows somebody" is in the "right place at the right time"—and walks off with your job.

Some people seem to have all the luck. True. Next time you can be one of them.

Whether you're just entering the work force or trying to move up through the corporate ranks...whether you want to maneuver a career change or start your own business...you can literally make your own luck by making the right connections.

Call it networking or "schmoozing," the ongoing process of building and maintaining personal and professional relationships through reciprocal communication and sharing information with individuals and groups of individuals can give you a powerful advantage in any marketplace.

This book will show you how.

It's a jungle out there

What else is new, right? Getting a job or doing business on your own means finding your way through a formidable tangle of information while fending off competition at every turn. Spend all your time and energy hacking away at the underbrush and you're likely to stray off your path—or be ambushed by a competitor. But step back and figure out what's going on out there—who has the power and the right information—and you're much more likely to reach your destination intact and ahead of the competition.

According to the U.S. Department of Labor, outplacement specialists and other employment experts, power lies in informal contacts. While it's difficult to take an accurate measurement, most agree that the majority of available jobs are filled through word-of-mouth referrals or tips from relatives, friends or acquaintances.

Now, picture your custom-tailored resume and cover letter slowly suffocating under a growing pile of paper on some hiring manager's desk. That is reality. Today's managers simply have less time, and more at stake. Most expect to spend one-and-a-half times your starting salary to recruit you and bring you up to speed, so they are understandably wary of taking a chance on someone they don't know.

Maybe you think that starting your own business will give you more control over your destiny. You're right. But know that you will be stepping into an arena in which the risks don't diminish until you've logged at least five years. And the competition for clients, even among one-person, home-based operations, is heating up on a *global* scale. Business owners need more than financing—they need emotional support, "inside" information and ongoing access to a range of resources.

Networking is the advantage you've been looking for

We want to assure you that it's not our intent to intimidate you or stifle your grand designs for the future. We happen to think women are some of the most innovative, gutsy corporate trailblazers and business owners around. In fact, you'll meet some of the best within the pages of this book.

These women share a common denominator: A dedication to active, ongoing networking. Over the years, they have learned that credentials, experience and sweat equity are no longer enough to ensure career progress. Now more than ever, who you know—and *who knows you*—determines your access to the opportunities you need to get ahead. They know that networking is not a cure-all—it's simply the best career and business leverage you can have.

The good news is that women are naturals

The average man may be reluctant to ask for help, but most women feel comfortable seeking other people out for support, information and resources. If you've ever asked a neighbor to refer a pediatrician or shared some fruit from the office grapevine, you were networking.

You may tap this informal information network for the contacts, leads and feedback you need to get a new client or your next job. But you won't reap the full rewards of networking until you begin to consistently build a web of connections—beginning with referrals from people in your inner circle.

Maybe you've grown accustomed to flying "solo," swooping down every now and then for a hit-or-miss referral. Maybe you're a dues-paying member of a professional association who is finding it difficult to move away from that old familiar wall during meetings. This book will help you take the first step, and then a second and third, until you begin to create and nurture the networking connections that will carry you toward your goals. Throughout your lifetime, you may be able to:

- Follow up on a job lead that will never be advertised or passed along to a headhunter.
- Increase your income (by more than $6,000 on average, according to a survey of the membership of the National Association for Female Executives (NAFE) in 1993).
- Get a promotion or increase your visibility within your company and industry.
- Build a client base for business.
- Manage increased responsibilities during downsizing.
- Brainstorm ideas, programs or concepts.
- Get financing to expand your small business.
- Find information that may be difficult to get through traditional channels.
- Get advice from experts.
- Develop new skills and expertise.
- Gain access to business services and training resources.

But isn't all of this just a little bit calculated?

If you've always shied away from name-dropping and business card-swapping events, your instincts are good. Not much will come from this kind of superficial effort, because networking is not designed to be a "quick fix" for a short-term problem.

Successful networking is a skill you can develop and use at any time, but you're investing in a reciprocal process that should take place over a lifetime. In fact, it breaks down for the people who dabble in it or misuse it.

If you're still wondering if this business of networking isn't a bit too calculated, a better question to ask yourself may be, can you afford *not* to network? Continued corporate downsizing and restructuring have made career footholds slippery at best. Experts predict that most of us can expect to make multiple job—and career—changes during our lifetimes. In the years ahead, the quality of your connections may well ensure your survival.

You won't gain ground standing on the sidelines

This roll-up-your-sleeves, hands-on workbook will guide you through the steps necessary to develop your own action plan. We'll explore your personal and business goals, and examine your existing network. (Don't worry, you have one, even if you don't yet think of it that way.)

Then we'll offer you a range of ideas for expanding your networking activity, and look at the roles your contacts can play—from coach to devil's advocate. You'll discover there are many different kinds of networking resources—from structured "leads groups" to informal support groups. We'll give you some guidelines for evaluating your networking options so you can make the most of your time and money.

With a basic plan of action, you'll be ready to incorporate networking strategies specific to either the corporate or business world. Through stories and anecdotes, we'll share with you the experiences of a diverse group of women.

Finally, the comprehensive reference section includes many business and women's groups that offer wide-ranging support, such as training and business and financial services. We think you'll find it a useful ongoing resource.

Appropriately, this book is being written as result of a networking relationship. As authors, we were co-editors of a consumer travel magazine during the 1980s. We became friends. We kept in touch.

Both of us have experienced the superficial sides of networking. Both are recipients of its incredible riches. But in talking with many other women like ourselves, we were astounded by the diversity of opportunities they have created through their energy and generosity.

We're confident that reading about their experiences—and ours—will help you place networking in a brand-new light. This book will help get involved in *the ongoing process of building and maintaining personal and professional relationships through reciprocal communication and sharing of information with individuals and groups of individuals.*

And then, some enchanted evening...or early morning or afternoon...you'll meet a stranger at a networking event, through a relative or even via an electronic bulletin board. Over time that person may become an employer, a client, a mentor, a friend. One day you may receive a call from out of the blue and an opportunity that may literally change the course of your life...or become the substance of your success. That's how it happens.

About six years ago, I was part of a marketing team charged with producing a brochure for an annual software users' conference. During one meeting, we reviewed the work of several graphic designers. An independent meeting planner had proposed three designers. I brought in a team I'd worked with in the past. By unanimous decision, my former colleagues got the job—and produced a beautiful brochure. They were just starting out in business, so it was a tremendous boost for them.

But that wasn't the end of the story. One of the three designers who didn't get the job impressed me as being very talented and accomplished. When I called her to tell her we had chosen someone else for that particular project, I took great care to tell her how much I thought of her presentation and her distinctive, elegant style. I also promised to keep her card. I did. In fact, I took it with me when I left the software company soon afterward to venture out on my own as a freelance writer. When I called, she very graciously took time to review my portfolio and then referred me to one of her clients, a company that is still my biggest account.

But there is still more. I have since teamed up with the design team we hired to produce the conference brochure on half a dozen jobs. A co-worker who sat in that initial design review also referred me to the decision-maker at the new company she had joined. And after I was in business for about a year, the meeting planner provided a glowing review of me to one of her clients, who turned into one of mine. Is it over?

Probably not.

—J

There is a magic about networking

We hope you'll discover and respect it. Even your best-laid plans can't anticipate the serendipity you're likely to encounter. When you are courteous and value everyone you meet, you'll find even seeds of your efforts that seem lost to the wind carry opportunities that have a way of blossoming at unexpected moments.

Only one thing is certain. The more seeds you plant, the richer your future possibilities. So let's get started.

Part 1

What is networking?

Chapter 1

The skill you didn't know you had

I stopped by to visit my friend Marcy the other day and, over coffee, launched into a complaint about my messy house. She whipped out a file from her kitchen desk, filled with flyers and notes about housecleaning services. "I haven't used this one," she said, "but Fran down the street says they're reasonable and they do a fantastic job." She commented on others, sharing information she'd gathered from friends as well as her own experiences. I walked away with a couple of names to call.

Over the past couple of months, Marcy has called me with names of potential clients, and faxed me various articles and bits of information—from a news release about the reorganization of a local business to a clip about a single man she thought I ought to pursue. In fact, she recently passed on the name of a potential interview source for this very book.

Marcy is the best networker I know. She's never attended a "how to work a room" seminar, she doesn't have the world's biggest business card collection and she doesn't join organizations just to fill up her calendar with breakfast and lunch meetings. But she clearly knows the secrets to successful networking. Although she and I are in different fields, if I were looking for work, Marcy would be one of the first people I'd call. Heck, I'd call Marcy first if I were looking for a plumber, a good deal on a computer or the best place in town to buy pastrami.

—B

We introduce our first chapter with this story in order to illustrate a very powerful premise: that networking is indeed *familiar, female* and *absolutely essential* for success in any endeavor—whether it's finding a house-cleaning service or landing a job. In our professional experiences, we too often run into women who believe that networking is something alien—an advanced business skill or a secret activity of the "good old boy" domain, carried on only in realms above the glass ceiling. But more than anything, we hear from women that networking is something they just don't feel comfortable doing.

We hope that, because you're reading this book, this isn't how you feel. But if you're harboring some doubt about the value of networking or your ability to be successful at it—this chapter will help convince you that Marcy is not an anomaly—that there are lots of Marcys out there successfully networking and that you, too, can build a powerful and effective networking system that will serve you for life.

Networking's wicked stepsister

Indeed, our perceptions of networking often take on a grim form. One woman described her expectations of a professional luncheon that she was loathe to attend:

"They're a bunch of wolves in sheep's clothing. As soon as I walk into that room of smiling strangers, they'll attack, eager to shake my hand, cram their business cards in my pocket and forget my name as soon as they realize I can't give them any business or a job."

Here are a few more colorful descriptions of networking we gathered from women.

- "Practicing your smile and handshake so you can 'work' cocktail parties and other functions."
- "Pestering people you don't know that well to get them to introduce you to people you don't know at all."
- "Something that requires an aggressive, pushy personality."

Yeesh! It's no wonder these women feel uncomfortable with the concept of networking. Who wants to think of themselves as using—or being used by—other people for their own selfish purposes? Women often avoid opportunities to network because it seems self-serving, exploitive—even unethical.

But that's not what networking is about. Later in this chapter, we'll dissect the definition of networking and show that respect, integrity, sharing and other positive concepts are important elements in networking successfully.

Today's workplace: uncertain and ever-changing

But first, let's examine some of the reasons that networking is fast becoming not just a skill for success, but a requirement for survival in the world of work. In a climate of dramatic shifting and upheaval, the survivors will be the proactive workers who can develop a solid foundation in this shaky workplace. Consider these major trends in the work force:

1. **Fewer jobs, less loyalty from corporate America.** The recession that triggered corporate downsizing, reorganizations and restructuring in the late 1980s and early '90s resulted in permanent changes in the work force. Despite upturns in the economy since, experts warn us that the millions of jobs lost during this time are not going to return. Big business continues to run lean and mean, and new jobs are being generated at a much slower rate than in past recoveries. The same corporations that used to award fat pensions to their employees at the end of long careers are not the harbors of job security they once were. Millions of Americans—blue-collar and white-collar alike—have been displaced by economic forces and continue to struggle to find their place in the work force.

2. **Fierce competition for fewer advancement opportunities.** Those who somehow survived the corporate shakeups and managed to cling to their jobs are confronted with change, too. Organizations are flattening out—no longer does the ladder of success climb very high. Management structures are changing, and the opportunities for traditional career advancement are slim. Fewer opportunities for promotion are available, and the competition for them is fierce.

3. **For women, the corporate ladder very often stops at the glass ceiling.** If competition weren't tough enough, women still have to contend with issues of discrimination. According to a 1995 study conducted by the federal Glass Ceiling Commission, women hold only 5 percent of the top management positions in American corporations. And in addition to glass ceilings, we have glass walls and glass doors to contend with. Certain traditionally "male" industries remain closed to women, and within companies, those departments or areas with the most influence and power are also tougher for women to break into.

4. **Growth in small and mid-sized businesses.** As major corporations remain static or downsize and look to outside sources for services, it will be small and mid-sized businesses that will benefit. Consequently, they will offer most of the job opportunities in the coming years. The Small Business Administration (SBA) projects

that businesses with fewer than 500 employees will create 70 per-cent of all new jobs in the nation's fastest-growing industries be-tween 1990 and 2005. Because these companies may not be as visible as traditional corporate giants, individuals who want to work for or with them may have to do a little more digging to find out about such opportunities.

5. **Growth in women-owned businesses.** Who's starting these new businesses? Women! As the number of small businesses continues to grow, the number of *women*-owned small businesses grows at an even greater rate. The SBA predicts that women will own 40 percent of small businesses by the year 2000. The number of busi-nesses owned or operated by women jumped 18 percent between 1991 and 1994, to 7.7 million, according to a national study con-ducted by Dun & Bradstreet Information Services and the National Foundation for Women Business Owners (NFWBO). This same study also revealed that employment among women-owned-and-operated businesses increased more than 11 percent during this same period, while employment among all American companies increased by less than half of this percentage.

The reasons given for this boom are numerous. Women are ex-periencing the limitations of corporate opportunities. Discouraged by what they view as little hope for advancement, feeling disen-franchised in a frequently inflexible environment, many women have decided to strike out on their own—and with great success! Statistics indicate that women-owned businesses may have a higher success rate than those run by men. As women continue to flex their entrepreneurial muscles, the American worker will find himself or herself increasingly employed by, selling to, negotiating with and conducting business with women.

6. **Job-hopping and career-hopping on the rise.** With the upheaval in the work force, career paths will take twists and turns that, in the past, might have been interpreted as signs of instability. The Bureau of Labor Statistics estimates that today's worker will change jobs an average of seven times in a working career. Other experts, like Joyce Schwarz, author of *Successful Recareering,* anticipate that individuals will change *careers* as many as seven times. Already, employers and human resources professionals are reporting that job-hopping, even career-hopping, is not considered

the negative situation it once was. In fact, as the demand for knowledge and experience broadens, such diverse experience is often viewed as a plus.

Bottom line, what all these changes mean is this: The worker of the future can't rely on the traditional methods of securing job or career success. A polished resume, flawless interviewing skills, expert closing techniques, hard work and a good attendance record won't necessarily cut it. Don't count on getting that promotion because you're next in line. You can't rely on getting that job because you meet all the criteria listed in the want ad. There's no guarantee you'll get the client's business because you've had it for the last 10 years. The responsibility is upon each of us—not some beneficent corporation or paternalistic employer—to build our own secure career foundation. And in order to do so, we must adopt new, more powerful tools. One of these essential tools is networking.

Some good news: a trend toward *female* management style

With the shift from an industrial economy to one that's information-based, there's been a change in the management style that's used to run American business. The traditional hierarchical structure was based on a military model. (It's been described in sports metaphors and even in paternalistic language as well.) The workers—the "troops" at the bottom—reported to a commander, who in turn reported to a higher commander until the structure reached the top. Within this structure, we were geared to take orders from our leaders—no questions asked. Information was not shared. Those of us at the bottom were to *do*, not think.

Today, a more effective model, described by many management gurus as *female*, is beginning to emerge. Because, indeed, this style exhibits characteristics that are traditionally attributed to women—supportive, flexible, people-oriented, sharing, open, creative, fostering individuality. In *Megatrends for Women,* authors John Naisbitt and Patricia Aburdene define women's leadership as the effective management style of the future.

What are some of the characteristics of this female-style management? While the traditional structure is described as a ladder or a pyramid, the new structure is depicted as a web, a lattice, even a network. The emphasis is on sharing information rather than concealing or controlling it. Empowering and facilitating rather than giving orders and directing. Team recognition rather than individual stardom. Collaboration rather than competition. Long-term vision rather than short-term results.

As Melissa Giovagnoli, author of *Make Your Connections Count: Your Six-Step System to Build Your MegaNetwork,* notes, men are often proprietary in their relationships. They're more likely to take the view "I've got this relationship and I want to keep it to myself." They don't want to share. But in the near future, Giovagnoli adds, the "people who will get jobs are the people who can create webs, and women are particularly adept at that."

Female management and the networking connection

Now, with this picture before us, let's revisit our definition of networking and look for some parallels between the networking process and this new "female" management style. We defined networking in the introduction as:

> *The ongoing process of building and maintaining personal and professional relationships through reciprocal communication and sharing of information with individuals and groups of individuals.*

1. **People orientation leads to building relationships.** The language we use to describe this new management style puts the emphasis on people and their relationships to one another. We use words and phrases like *empowering, connecting, team-oriented* and *motivating,* and remove from our vocabulary such terms as *rank, control, order* and *direct.* Indeed, our management and work philosophies are acknowledging that most valuable of resources—people power—and are becoming more relationship-oriented.

   Just as good management is now seen as a web of strengths, good networking requires the building of relationships, not just the making of contacts. At one point, we even considered titling this book *The Smart Woman's Guide to Relationships,* although we knew it would lead our readers to expect a different focus—one in which we claim no expertise. But the fact is, networking really is about relationships. They may not be romantic relationships, family relationships or even friendships, but they are relationships based on mutual interests and goals.

   As we interviewed business professionals, women and men who are considered to be networkers *par excellence,* we were surprised to discover how many of them bristled at the mention of the word "networking." Once we explained our definition of networking and brought up the phrase "relationship-building," most seemed to relax and expressed support for building and maintaining relationships that are mutually supportive.

In his book, *How to Use People to Get What You Want and Still Be a Nice Guy!: A Guide to Networking Know-How*, Les Garnas makes the distinction between gathering contacts and making connections. The difference is that connections are what contacts become when a relationship is built. And just as it's important for a good manager to nurture his or her employees, it's crucial for a good networker to cultivate solid relationships.

2. **Long-term vision leads to an ongoing process**—especially when it comes to people. When businesses confront the skyrocketing costs of hiring and training new employees, the importance of investing in a labor force that's going to stick around for awhile becomes quite clear.

   Likewise, networking requires a long-term outlook. Your efforts at networking don't end when you finally land that job or when you file business cards in your Rolodex following an industry luncheon. Networking takes nurturing. The seeds you carefully plant, tend, water and weed are more likely to bear fruit than those you scatter and ignore. As networking expert Dr. Ivan R. Misner describes in his new book, *The World's Best Known Marketing Secret: Building Your Business with Word-of-Mouth Marketing,* networking is more akin to farming than hunting. You want to *grow* your networking connections, not go in for the kill.

   Networking is not a quick-fix, short-term solution to a shortage of clients, the loss of a job or efforts to land a promotion. It requires a long-term commitment but promises a lifetime harvest of valuable support, connections and friendships.

3. **Sharing information leads to reciprocity and mutual support.** Openness is a key to the new management style. Information is shared, questions are encouraged and control is often given away. Managers look to offer reward and recognition, just as they seek employee commitment and support.

   Networking is not a one-sided venture either. Enhanced by mutual interest, it is indeed a give-and-take relationship. A genuine interest in sharing and communication is a prerequisite for effective networking. You don't withhold information on a job lead from your friend in Women in Communications, Inc. (WICI) because she hasn't done anything for you lately. You don't introduce your graphic designer to a potential client because you hope to get a big discount on your next job. You share information and offer support whenever you can, because you have a relationship with that individual.

Women: the progenitors of the modern networking movement

We hope that, by illustrating the connection between the characteristics of female-style leadership and networking, we've overcome any doubt you may have that women are *natural networkers*. But if you're still not convinced, consider this: Women are credited with having catalyzed the modern networking movement. Misner points to the growth of women-owned business in the 1970s and '80s as the beginnings of organized networking.

Women business owners, Misner says, got together to provide professional contacts to one another as well as the support they weren't receiving in the corporate world. "I think women felt that there was some magic going on behind the doors in these good-old-boy networks. And they decided to start their own groups—and created something much better. They ended up creating organizations that were much more focused." In his book, Misner says, "These groups were created not as service clubs, but as *bona fide* networking organizations. Many had no pretenses; the members were there to network, and everything else was secondary."

More good news: Women match men in networking success

Misner notes that, as women in the work force are increasing in number and influence, the necessity for women's networking groups may be diminishing. Most of the service organizations, such as Rotary International and Kiwanis International, now accept women into their ranks. And leads groups experience equal participation from women and men. He notes that nearly 50 percent of the directors for Business Network Intl., a leads group he founded, are women.

In fact, based on the results of his doctoral dissertation, which studied the number of referrals received and percentage of business closed in leads groups, women don't appear to be hobbled by either personality differences or inequities in the business world. When it comes to getting leads and turning them into business, he reports, "Women and men are running neck and neck. There are no discernible differences in their success."

Melissa Giovagnoli echoes Misner's point. "I would be so bold as to say this: Because of socialization, women's place has been in the home, but now that's shifted. Women are multi-taskers, and that ability is the setup for networks. They will outdo men tenfold. We have only begun to see what women can do."

Conclusion

There's a memorable scene in the comic movie *For Love or Money*, in which Michael J. Fox plays the part of a hotel concierge who also happens to be a networking master. In the scene, Fox ducks into a helicopter owned by a man named Chuck, who has made it available to Fox.

Curious about Fox's connections, the helicopter pilot yells over the loud chop of the propellers, "How do you know Chuck?"

"I *don't* know Chuck," Fox yells back. "But I know Eddie Shackner. Eddie knows Jerry Levine, Jerry knows George Spitzer. *George* knows Chuck."

"Small world!" the pilot replies. In fact, networking *can* shrink the world. And by establishing mutually beneficial connections between yourself and others, more of what the world has to offer will be available to you.

But a strong web of relationships doesn't just happen. As Misner points out in his book, "It's not net-*sit* or net-*eat*. It's net*work*." Successful networking does take effort, along with a certain degree of skill and confidence. And that's what we hope this book will offer you, through the information, tips, skill-building exercises and personal anecdotes included in the following chapters.

As women, we've always known how important relationships are—in our communities and with our neighbors, families and partners. In this arena, we've served successfully as peacekeepers, matchmakers, fence-menders, role models, supporters, confidants and allies. And despite our short history as significant players in the work force, we are rapidly discovering that these relationship-building skills can be transferred into the business realm. Just like Dorothy in *The Wizard of Oz,* we've had the power within us all along.

Chapter 2

What does it take to be a successful networker?

Good bone structure, like many things in life, is something you're either born with, or you're not. But the beauty of networking is that it's *not* such a gift. True, some people are naturally adept at making connections, but having been born with the personality of a talk-show host is not a requirement for becoming a successful networker. Nor do you have to have a computer-like brain to store all the names of people you've ever been introduced to. With commitment and purpose, anyone can develop effective networking skills.

And there's more good news: Many of the traits that experts identify as crucial to successful networking tend to be the characteristics typically identified as "female"—the qualities pinpointed by management pros as indicative of the new female management style. So you may have more of an edge than you imagined. Let's consider some of the key characteristics that make a successful networker:

A successful networker is...

1. **Committed.** The "c" word, again. (But in this context, *you* may be the one who is squeamish about making a commitment to networking on a regular basis!) Once you accept the premise that networking is a way of life, it's obvious that it requires a long-term commitment. Developing a web of relationships is an ongoing process. Not only is it necessary to commit to a networking philosophy, it's essential to devote a certain amount of time and energy as well.

   We're not talking about back-breaking work or around-the-clock accountability. There will be many times when you will step forward to get involved in activities such as structured mentoring programs or fund-raising events. But even more important than these short-term stints is your long-term behavior.

Will you make an effort to stay in touch with your contacts? Are you willing to regularly set aside time to call people on a regular basis, schedule lunches, send off quick notes, fax interesting articles, whip off e-mail messages and focus on the concerns of your connections? If so, your network will flourish. If you let these relationships go, if you fail to be there for others, your network will eventually go to seed.

The advice of Terrie Williams, who built a successful public relations agency representing some of the world's best-known entertainment and sports figures largely on the strength of her networking connections, bears repeating: "It's important to be in touch with people, not just when you want or need something. If you haven't stayed in touch and then just send a note when something good happens to them, it's going to be really obvious."

2. **More interested in *giving* than getting.** Truth is, we're all in it—whatever *it* is—for ourselves. Most of what we do in life is somehow connected to "WIIFM": "What's In It For Me?" And that's okay. But in order to *get* anything out of networking, you've got to learn to put your personal interests on the back burner, and focus your energies on others' needs and goals as well. It's a sort of "Do unto others" philosophy found at the core of many spiritual beliefs.

A good networker can find hundreds of ways to give: Referrals, informational interviews, encouragement and feedback. As you graduate to more senior status through networking, you'll be able to give more. But wherever you are, you already have a lot to give. Too many women are willing to contribute, but don't believe they have anything of value to give.

"When I was asked to be a mentor, I thought, 'I wonder what I can offer,' " admits Sandra Borrer-Jury, a Philadelphia-based consultant, when pursued to become involved in a program sponsored by the Philadelphia Women's Network. "I learned that I had more to offer than I thought."

Susan Hailey, director of business development and planning for Resumix, a Silicon Valley software company, has a positive feeling about the value of what she has to offer others. "I get great delight from giving advice to people," she says. "I have a healthy ego, and I really care—I want to be helpful. I want to steer others in ways that are really good for them, so they make really good choices."

3. **A good listener.** Being a good listener is more than smiling, nodding and interjecting an occasional "uh-huh" when others talk to you. Good networking requires *real* listening—reading between the lines. Hearing a business acquaintance remark about problems with a vendor and responding with horror stories of your own is one way to listen. But following up with a couple of names of reliable vendors you've worked with shows you're really listening. Responding with enthusiasm when a former co-worker expresses interest in a local company is one level of listening. Faxing your friend a few recent news clips, or introducing her to the human resources director at that company, is a more advanced level. Fine-tune your listening skills for powerful networking: Instead of simply acknowledging the problem, try to provide solutions.

4. **Curious.** When interacting with others, a good networker—using her excellent listening skills—hears clues that stimulate interest and offer opportunities to explore further. Without the element of curiosity, your networking conversations may often drop with a thud after you establish what the individual does and where he or she works. But a curious networker will probe further. "You provide a gift-basket and flower delivery service targeted to businesses? What was it in your background that led you to this career path? What would you say really launched your business? What sort of company do you find makes the best customer for your service?"

    Curiosity need not come off as nosiness or offensive probing. When approached with sincerity, expressing a genuine interest in someone else will most often result in a positive—and reciprocal—response. Generally, people appreciate this sort of attention and, as a result, react by opening up, sharing information and being more interested in *you*.

5. **Ready to follow up.** Too often, "Let's do lunch," or "I'll look into that for you," doesn't mean much. In fact many of us have probably had the experience of running into a casual business acquaintance frequently, always to conclude a brief exchange with, "We really have to get together soon." And that's the last we hear of it. An important rule of successful networking is, if you say you're

going to do something—*do it*. Whether it's scheduling lunch or passing on some information, follow through with your commitment, so that your networking connections come to know you as someone who does what she says.

At the very least, follow up with a call. "Ellen, I told you I'd let you know if I knew of anyone looking for a graphic designer. I thought I could come up with a couple of names but it seems no one's looking right now. I'll let you know if things change." An addendum to this rule: Follow up *when* you say you will—if you promise you'll call tomorrow, be sure that you do.

Further, doing *more* than you say you will is the key to real success in the networking lifestyle. A friend expresses dissatisfaction about his job. He hasn't asked you to do anything—other than to commiserate over a beer. But the sign of a good listener and a good "follower-upper" is response even when not asked. You send him information about a workshop in his field. You introduce him to a contact who may be hiring. You touch base with him, regularly, just to see if the status has changed.

6. **Able to ask for help.** Yes, we know, the stereotype is that *men* are the ones who can never admit they need help. They won't stop to ask for directions, or give up tinkering with the kitchen sink until emergency flood conditions require a call to the plumber.

But plenty of women, too, are often reluctant to admit that they can't handle something themselves—particularly in the work arena. While we're often willing to go out of our way to help others, we frequently find it difficult to ask for assistance ourselves, as evidenced by Susan Hailey's remarks: "The 'taking' has always felt a little bit uncomfortable. I have always been highly available in a giving role and people have really used me in that way. I have had to learn how to get very comfortable with taking from that network."

The ability to ask others for help is crucial to successful networking. Whether it's requesting advice, information or an introduction to an important contact, you'll need to be able to make your needs clear. You can't count on networking contacts to intuit what you need. If you merely "hint" to your co-worker that you'd really like to work in marketing, he may not guess that what you *mean* is that you wish he'd introduce you to his pal, the director of the marketing department.

"I'm shocked at how many people never really say what they want," says networking pro Melissa Giovagnoli. "If there's anything that women need to do better, it's ask for more." Laura Gates, owner of the public relations and marketing firm, The Gates Group, agrees, "Knowing what kind of information, support or referrals you want is the first step. But then you must ask for it in so many words. Are you looking for a job? Say, 'Hi, my name is Laura Gates. I just moved here from New York and I'm looking for a job in PR.' Then someone might say, 'Oh, you know my aunt Clara has a PR firm.' "

If you've built relationships based on mutual support with your networking connections, it's entirely appropriate for you to *ask* for help. And most people are appreciative of the opportunity to help an individual they have a positive relationship with.

7. **Able to brag.** Now, here's the tough one. Most career experts observe that women have more difficulty than men in feeling comfortable about "tooting their own horn." In fact, even when recognized for their accomplishments, women frequently respond with comments such as, "Oh, it was no big deal," or "Well, it wasn't really my idea."

A good networker *must* learn to be comfortable with sharing her achievements. No, we're not implying that you should monopolize every conversation with your exploits and bore everyone to tears with your successes. But it is essential to let your networking connections know what you're doing and what you've accomplished. You may be a charming lunch companion, but if your fellow members at your professional association don't *know* you've: a) landed a prestigious account, b) achieved record sales in your industry or c) won an important award, how will they know that you truly are an exemplary businessperson, one to recommend to others?

Take credit. Don't share your success, then blush and pass on the credit to your co-workers, boss or, worse, luck. Be proud, not pompous, about your achievements and spread the news. This allows your contacts to learn not just about what you do, but *how* you do it—with excellence!

8. **A consumer of knowledge.** While networking is indeed about relationships, reading up on your profession, your community and
the business community in general is going to give you an edge in
developing those relationships. By keeping abreast of events,
you'll know where to seek out effective networking connections. If
you haven't already, develop a voracious appetite for information.
Read avidly. Hop aboard the Internet.

On the average, Terrie Williams scours seven newspapers a
day. And not just the front page news. "Read the society page to
know who's doing what with whom," she advises. "If you want to
go after some business and you notice that someone is engaged or
has gotten married, you can acknowledge something personal."

You may also save your business. *"The New York Times* had
an article the other day on home-based businesses legislation,"
Thérèse Watley told us. As director of Home-Based Entrepreneur
Network (HEN), she attests that this kind of information is crucial
to her membership. "You might not feel that it affects you," she
says, "but someday a neighbor may call the zoning board to investigate your business, and you may be shut down because you
didn't know you were operating outside the local zoning laws."

If nothing else, between your accomplishments and today's
news, you'll always have something to talk about.

9. **Courageous.** It can be scary to do something new—whether it's
braving a bungee jump, changing your hairstyle or walking into a
room full of strangers. While networking situations aren't always
ones that provoke sweaty palms or somersaulting stomachs, it does
require occasional stretching—reaching out to new individuals,
perhaps joining an organization where you know no one or
(shudder) speaking before a group of strangers.

It takes a certain amount of courage to network well. Recognize
that discomfort may accompany you in some networking situations, but don't let it hold you back.

Consider using Andra Brack's strategy when introducing yourself to new people. An executive director of leads organization
Business Network Intl. (BNI), she explains that when she feels intimidated about introducing herself to new people, she uses her
"CIPHY" ("Can I Possibly Help You?") approach. "If I think about
what I can do to help someone else—instead of thinking about

what they can do for me—it makes it easier for me to approach someone I don't know."

As you feel a little bolder, try going solo to a networking event. When you're surrounded by an entourage of co-workers, friends and associates, it's difficult to extend yourself to meet new people. All of us have attended an event where we sat at a table with our co-workers. No doubt, we had a great time, complained about the chicken, applauded the speech and returned to work...without meeting anyone new.

According to Dr. Frank Farley, a University of Wisconsin psychologist who's studied risk-takers for 30 years, you define yourself and add to your self-esteem and self-confidence with every risk you take. With practice, you may surprise yourself at how easy it becomes to reach out to people you don't know.

10. **Able to remember.** Yes, remembering names is important to effective networking. But when you're forced to admit that you've forgotten the name of someone you know you've met, approaching him or her with a genuine smile can work magic and pave the way for forgiveness.

What's even more impressive than remembering names is remembering details about a conversation you may have had. Try approaching someone at a luncheon or event with a smile and comment reflecting a previous interaction: "Oh, I've been wondering since we last talked how your fund raiser finally turned out," or "Last time we met, you were getting ready to send your daughter to college. How are you coping with an empty nest?" Chances are the individual won't even notice whether you used his or her name. Remembering the details about an individual is one of the most effective ways to transform a casual introduction into a solid connection.

11. **Patient.** "What goes around comes around." "You never know what the future will bring." These are the mantras of successful networkers.

"It's not a quickie thing," emphasizes Lya Sorano, director of the Atlanta Women in Business. "Coming to one meeting and then going home and saying, 'I never get anything out of it,' means you came with the wrong expectation. You really have to regard it as an investment that you are making. It takes a while to build up contacts." Andra Brack advises new members of BNI that they may have to put in a year of weekly meetings before they see a strong payoff in networking-generated business.

But, somewhere down the road, patient networkers are guaranteed to reap the benefits of their efforts. Networking can pay off in the development of a lasting friendship, as a referral to someone who can fix your house or as a lead for a business opportunity.

12. **Courteous.** Your mom was right. "Please" and "thank you" are magic words. A good networker no doubt goes through boxes of thank-you notes more quickly than most people. But more than that, she acknowledges the kind deeds of others on the spot—and often. Perhaps you've been surprised yourself by grateful associates who've pulled you aside to offer appreciation. "Hey, thanks for the introduction. I've been trying to meet that officer for months now." Or "You can't imagine what a favor you've done for me. I had no idea XYZ company was reorganizing until you told me. This is a perfect time for me to call on them." Responses like these tend to garner further acts of helpfulness and create an overall sense of goodwill.

It's about as basic as a Robert Fulghum manual: Treat everybody, regardless of perceived status, with the same respect. Return phone calls promptly. Spell people's names correctly. Don't monopolize conversations. Be nice to assistants and receptionists (you'd be surprised at how much power they have). Apologize when you make mistakes.

13. **Involved.** A good networker is involved—not just in the networking process or with her job, but in everything she commits herself to. She doesn't limit her involvement in group memberships to paying dues once a year. She's the woman who attends most of the meetings, raises her hand and asks questions of the speakers, stays afterward or arrives early to discuss concerns or ideas with the group leaders. She volunteers for committee work and planning.

Involvement—not mere affiliation—is a key to networking success. You're better off joining *two* organizations and becoming active in those, than being on the rosters of seven groups that you don't have time for.

14. **A believer in what she does.** Alice Ostrower, teacher at the Entrepreneurial Center of Hartford College for Women (Connecticut)

and an executive director for BNI, has been described as "the Barnum of networking." A staunch believer in the joys of networking, she warns, however, that you can't succeed at it if you aren't comfortable with yourself and what you do. "You can't be a good networker pitching something that you don't believe in. Once you love what you're doing, it's easy to tell other people about it."

It goes back to integrity. If you're selling snake oil and you *know* it won't cure a thing, it's going to be very difficult for you to get out there and peddle it to others.

Conclusion

Please note that our list of ideal networking characteristics does not include terms like "social," "talkative," "outgoing" or "aggressive." That's because there isn't one special personality type that fits the profile of a good networker. There are shy, reserved individuals who've woven an expansive web of networking contacts, and there are smiling, glad-handers who flit from one function to another, operating on a networking foundation about as solid as a sandcastle. *Anyone* who is dedicated to becoming an effective networker can learn and use the traits covered in this chapter.

Chapter 3

Networking connections: Where do they come from?

My first job out of college was as the editor of a bimonthly magazine showcasing restaurants and entertainment for business travelers to a major Midwestern city. After a few months, however, my enthusiasm for my job was doused by serious organizational problems beyond my control.

One day, my college professor, in town visiting an old friend, called me for lunch. After listening to my complaints, he urged me to contact the editor of a trade magazine in another city who had an opening for an assistant editor. I was surprised. What about sticking this out for six more months? "Nonsense," he said. "Make the call." I returned from an all-day interview with a job offer in hand.

—J

- Laurie learned of a job opening on a corporate magazine from *another parent in her child's class.* The editor who interviewed her initially favored another candidate, but the personal reference from a mutual acquaintance convinced her to hire Laurie.

- John credited landing a big account for his fledgling public relations agency to an introduction from a *former co-worker.*

- Jennifer, new to the city, brings in most of her new printing accounts through leads from her membership in a *business referral group* that meets once a week.

- Nina, a self-employed accountant, landed a new client when *another client* recommended her at a happy hour.

- Julie, with a master's degree in special education, was the first to hear of a job opening at a head injury clinic. *Her mother,* a volunteer for the clinic, found out about the opening as she typed up a personnel request form for the human resources department.

• After launching her marketing business, Lois received valuable advice regarding taxes and other start-up issues from her *online friends* who communicated via a small-business bulletin board.

Co-workers. Organizations. Neighbors and friends. Cyberspace contacts. Clients. Even Mom.

What these few examples illustrate is that there is no single source for career contacts—there is no exclusive, inaccessible society of networkers. Potential is everywhere—and *you,* social female creature that you are, are probably already well hooked-in to the various sources available for tapping. In this chapter, we'll identify some categories of networking sources you may not have considered. But before we begin, let's review an important point.

Diversify your networking

Just as in investing, diversification is the key to networking success. You can't expect to meet every career need by putting all your eggs in one basket. You may find family, friends and maybe a community group an adequate base of contacts when hunting for that first job, but as your career path twists, turns, detours and branches out in multiple directions, you'll need to tap into different types of resources and information. Professional organizations, service organizations, co-workers and other business relationships may play a greater—or lesser—role in your networking web, depending on where you are in your career cycle.

The important thing is to build a strong foundation that will support you through the various stages of career growth—and this means you need to diversify your contacts.

Additionally, in order to have as strong a foundation as possible, it's important to build slowly and carefully—stressing *quality* over quantity. Remember, networking is more than a singular action that gets you a job, a client, ahead. Networking is an ongoing process, a mind-set. Your career needs will change as you grow professionally. As you consider potential connections, don't think in terms of the *now,* but rather in terms of laying the groundwork for a successful networking lifestyle.

So while we are going to bombard you with potential networking sources in this chapter, we're not suggesting you immediately attack them all, assaulting them with business cards, resumes and requests for help. Instead, we hope you'll use this as a reference, a catalyst to get you thinking about the connections you already have and areas in which you need to build.

To provide a structure for our exploration of networking sources, we'll break them down into four broad categories: *personal* contacts, *community* contacts, *professional* contacts and *online* contacts.

The personal you

Personal contacts are identified by two factors: You know these individuals on a *one-on-one basis*, and you know them in a *noncareer* capacity. These people know *you*, the daughter; *you*, the neighbor who never gets her recycling bin out in time for pickup; or *you*, the woman with the hair that won't take a perm. You may know these connections intimately (your mom, for example) or you may know them very superficially (your hairdresser). Either way, they offer a lot of networking potential.

Family

My grandmother had a habit of inserting herself into the lives of her grandchildren in irritating ways—like the time she bought three hideous ballgowns for $5 each at a garage sale and insisted that her granddaughters wear them to their proms. But her intimate knowledge of all aspects of our lives sometimes paid off, as it did for me one summer after my sophomore year of college when I desperately needed a "real" job. Her canasta buddy, Rosemary, was the manager of some department at a large insurance company. She convinced Rosemary to hire me, sight unseen. (I still suspect poor Rosemary must have lost one game too many to Grandma.) To this day, I'm not exactly sure what I did there—it involved a lot of unstapling, stamping and restapling of papers. But I earned a decent income, garnered a recommendation that served me in the future and had my first taste of corporate culture—which included an intimate knowledge of timeclocks.

—B

You may be past the point in your work life where a mere phone call from Dad to a close buddy will land you a job. But don't discount the members of your family as networking resources. (Both of us owe a few additional royalties to the efforts of our moms, who shamelessly promoted our previous books to friends, local schools and libraries.) They are perhaps more aware of your personal, social and career aspirations than most. Because of this, they can often provide you with valuable information, contacts and, of course, emotional support.

Obviously, if you have family members who are in the same field or a related area of business, their value as networking contacts may be even greater. Uncle Bob's a photographer and you're starting up a catering business? This could be the start of a beautiful relationship—he can refer you to his wedding clients and you can share your bar mitzvah schedule with him! Be sure to keep your relatives informed of your business aspirations, however. As family members, they're still likely to see you as "little Susie who always liked to host tea parties." You need to remind them that you're "all grown up."

Friends

As you progress in your career, it's likely that more of your friends will be co-workers or people in your industry, and these connections will be your most obvious networking buddies. But consider your neighbors, your exercise pal, your college roommate as valuable networking contacts as well. Among friends, it's surprisingly simple to bridge the gap between personal lives and career concerns. Because you have divergent circles of business contacts, friends can provide information and valuable connections that can help broaden opportunities for the both of you.

Don't overlook mere acquaintances, either. They may not be people you invite over for pizza. But the neighbor you commiserate with about the late delivery of the Sunday paper, or the woman from the gym who always seems to be on the StairMaster next to you may prove to have more in common with you than you'd expect. So seek out opportunities to strike up conversations and broaden your familiarity with these individuals.

Consumer connections

These are individuals you know through a noncareer capacity, however the contact comes through *their* career—in other words, they're people like your doctor, insurance agent, mechanic or hairdresser. (See Chapter 6 for a more complete list.) Most likely, they know more about *you* than you know about them, but only about one narrow aspect—your hair, your teeth, your carburetor. The value of these connections is that they come into contact with a lot people from various walks of life. And they may have information and connections that could prove helpful to you.

Obviously, you are in a position to help these contacts—as a client or patient, you are familiar with their service and can recommend others to them. And frequently, some service providers—insurance or real estate agents, for example—expect referrals from customers. (If you've ever bought insurance or a set of Ginsu knives, you've probably been asked for the names of other "intelligent consumers like yourself who would appreciate the exceptional value of this product.") Especially when you are pleased with their service, and they enjoy you as a client, you've got the makings of a great networking relationship!

The community you

Despite your work and the demands of your personal life, chances are you're in some way, great or small, involved in the bigger picture. Whether through the PTA or a class at the community college, you undoubtedly have contacts with the greater world through some sort of organized community involvement that's not related to your career. Consider this *small* sampling of potential connections:

- Church or synagogue attendance
- Committee work in church or synagogue
- Scout programs
- Youth sports
- PTA
- School involvement, such as class mother, fund raisers
- Social action—involvement in soup kitchens, recycling efforts
- Political activity
- Community causes
- Ski club
- Basketball league
- Classes
- Community centers such as YMCAs, JCCs, Girls Clubs, etc.
- Neighborhood or homeowner associations
- Cultural or art societies

These affiliations are ripe with networking potential—as long as you're *involved*. The mere act of paying your PTA dues or joining a church will not result in networking contacts. Getting active on a committee, planning an event or becoming an officer, even attending regularly, will. Why? Because this sort of involvement creates an ongoing connection rather than a one-time effort (there's the *commitment* aspect of networking, again!).

The other advantage of proactive involvement in a community organization is this: Because such groups often simulate a work environment, you have a chance to see others in action as well as showcase your own skills and talents. For example, you're on a committee planning a school fund-raising event. Although you've only known Millie through carpooling, you discover she's a relentless phone solicitor and has the motivational skills of Zig Ziglar. And *she* knows you're a tireless worker and an eloquent speech-giver—fodder for future referrals.

Finally, because the individuals are affiliated by personal interest, you'll certainly discover strong common ground. Whether you join a church, sign up for a music class or become active in a social cause, you'll meet other people who share your beliefs, values or interests. You're in contact with a *group* of people with convictions or interests similar to yours—offering greater connection potential.

The professional you

Clearly, professional connections may offer the most opportunities for relationships that lead to career advantages. But, too often, we only recognize one or two sources—co-workers or professional groups, for example. Following are some obvious and not-so-obvious sources for professional connections.

Co-workers

Many of your co-workers may overlap into the "friend" category. You work closely with them, share personal lives, meet for "happy hour." But whether they're intimate confidants or occasional lunch buddies, co-workers are valuable networking resources. Those you work with on a day-to-day basis can offer support, share insights, even teach you new skills.

Consider, too, those employees who work in other departments or even outside offices—and at different levels. These people can fill you in on current corporate gossip, let you know of changes and developments in their areas, even inform you of new opportunities if you're looking to make a change. And don't discount bosses and staff who report to you, as well. These relationships provide opportunities to establish mentoring relationships and more.

Co-workers don't lose their value as networking connections once they become *former* co-workers—in fact, they just might become more valuable. If they leave the company, you've just broadened your contact sphere—they're out there discovering new information and developing new networking connections. If you leave the company—say, to start your own business—they can still provide you with support and information, and perhaps even business down the road.

Vendors and clients

At first, a vendor-client relationship may seem a little one-sided; after all, one is always in the position of giving and the other receiving a service or product. Like some of the service providers among your personal connections, vendors typically expect clients who are pleased with their service to refer them to others, or to provide them with names of potential clients they might approach. But these relationships have a valuable networking aspect that goes beyond the traditional referral expectation. Whether you're the vendor or the client, whether your relationship is based on providing a service, consultation or product, you have a chance to build a relationship that will serve you beyond the clearly defined connection you have now.

For instance? Say you work with a printer to produce your company newsletter. You might learn from your printer about new technologies that allow you to put out a more sophisticated publication—more quickly—thus impressing your boss and paving the way for advancement. Your printer might connect you with other reliable vendors you need to produce the newsletter, such as designers and writers. The printer may tell you about his other clients—offering valuable community and industry information. You, on the other hand, provide him with a perspective of your business, which he can certainly apply to other clients. You may also put him into contact with other support people—writers, designers—you've worked with successfully. In addition, you may make him aware of developments in your company, which could provide further business opportunities for him.

And, if either of you are in a position to consider moving on, you may provide each other with job leads and helpful contacts.

Competitors

What? Consort with the enemy? Isn't that as implausible as an alliance between Pepsi and Coke? Quite the contrary! Connections with people who work for competitors of your company—or, if you're self-employed, who do the same thing you do—can be quite lucrative. As Melissa Giovagnoli, author of *Make Your Connections Count*, says: "In general, people fear there's not enough to go around. I have an abundance mentality. There is a lot of opportunity out here."

When I first set out on my own as a writer and editor, I was delighted to get a call from a travel industry publication asking if I could take on a feature assignment with a pretty tight deadline. I discovered they called me because a former co-worker, Julie, a self-employed writer like me, gave them my name when she was unable to accept the assignment. Both Julie and I continue to be kept busy by assignments from this magazine. And there have been times when I've had to decline an assignment, and I, in turn, gave the editor the names of other writers—my "competitors," if you will.

—B

Networking with the enemy almost always works out to be a productive tactic. And in most cases, it results in benefits for both parties. Who can better understand the challenges and problems you face than someone who does the same thing? In the corporate world, information (nonproprietary, of course) shared by like companies can prove valuable. And for the self-employed, such connections may result in the sharing of work overflow or referrals from competitors who may find a project doesn't quite "fit."

Professional organizations

Typically devoted to a single industry, such as accounting or nursing, these organizations allow individuals to meet and build relationships with others in their field. Known as knowledge networks, a term introduced in *Megatrends* by author John Naisbitt, these organizations are valuable for sharing of industry information, trends and ideas, and providing education.

Most of these organizations, such as Women In Communications, Inc. (WICI), and National Ad Directors Club, are national or even international in scope, but have local chapters. This permits members to get to know others through regular meetings, awards dinners, community service activities, events and more. Generally, dues are charged, which may support special events, newsletters, training programs and speakers.

Whether you're seeking professional development so you can be a greater asset to your company, or you're just entering the field and want to make contacts, professional organizations are great places to build a sturdy networking foundation. Most companies recognize the value of such organizations, and many are willing to pay membership dues and allow employees time off to attend meetings. In addition, professional groups can be sources of business and job leads, as many of them have developed official job-search programs.

A sampling of existing associations that serve general business interests is included in the resource section of this book. But the best source for information for both general business and profession-specific associations is the *Encyclopedia of Associations*. It also includes information about local chapters. Look for the publication in the reference section of your library.

Referral organizations

Generating leads for members is the singular purpose of these types of groups. While some may offer newsletters and occasional training programs, they exist solely to provide business for members. Your worst networking nightmare? A blizzard of business cards, glad-handing, back-patting and lead-feeding? Before you reject the idea, consider how, when based on a philosophy of relationship-building, such a group can be an effective networking outlet.

Take Business Network Intl. (BNI), for example. Nationwide, its chapters run similarly structured weekly meetings: Member are allowed a 60-second introduction in which to speak about themselves and their business. One member is "spotlighted," in a 10-minute presentation, which offers a more in-depth perspective of his or her business. A basket is passed around to gather leads that are distributed to the appropriate members, and these leads are then tracked so the organization can boast its impressive figures of more than 245,000 referrals and more than $85 million worth of business generated a year.

But what's really behind those figures, according to the organization's spokespeople, is its philosophy that "givers gain" and that long-term commitment works. BNI requires regular attendance from members, with the belief that only through getting to know each other can members genuinely and effectively support each other's business efforts.

Andra Brack, executive director for the Indiana region, explains: "BNI is structured the way it is because it works. The meetings and the frequency allow members to really get to know each other. We try to make members understand that they must be committed for the long haul in order for it to work. It may take up to a year to get a decent stream of leads from your involvement in BNI. But you can be sure you'll be getting good leads."

The Leads Club is another national networking group. Its founder, Ali Lassen, started the group for women because they were not permitted membership in such groups as Rotary International. Today, nearly 40 percent of the chapters remain women-only. Approximately 1 percent are men-only, and the rest are now mixed. According to Leads Club president Lisa Bentson, chapters keep their maximum number of members to 30. "Large is not necessarily better," she says, explaining that this allows more time for each member to provide in-depth focus to their business.

Both the Leads Club and BNI carefully qualify their membership, requiring references for admission. This way, there's less chance that an unscrupulous person will join. In addition, if any instances of poor service or bad business practices are reported from one of the referrals, they are investigated.

Such referral organizations that are based on relationship-building and integrity are likely to provide valuable contacts for most businesspeople. (Although Brack points out that some professions, pharmaceutical sales, for example, just don't garner much business through this type of affiliation.) In the northside Indianapolis chapter of BNI, a range of professions are represented, from the traditional (insurance agent, financial planner, lawyer) to the unusual (fortune cookie maker). A little more than half of the members are self-employed, while the bulk of the others are in sales. Members who have recently moved and have few contacts in their new location are particularly vocal about the benefits.

Typically, business lead organizations charge membership fees, averaging approximately $200 a year. One BNI member, owner of a fax services business, observes that the membership more than paid for itself with the first referral she received after joining.

BNI and the Leads Club addresses are listed in the resource section in this book.

Service organizations

While their primary purpose is to serve the communities in which they exist, service organizations are included in the "professional" category, because membership is defined by occupation rather than personal status. Typically, you join as Jane Doe, corporate accountant, rather than Jane Doe, concerned mother and neighbor.

Despite the emphasis on community service, most of these organizations do identify the networking opportunity as an important membership benefit. Indeed, many companies, recognizing the business value of such affiliations, pay for employee memberships—and often require their employees, especially those who rely upon referrals, to join such organizations. Membership is often restricted to one representative in a particular field.

Service organizations typically support specific community causes or charities—such as a children's hospital—through a variety of fund-raising activities. This affords the same networking opportunities as does other community involvement. You become involved in a worthwhile cause, often in a capacity that showcases your business skills, working closely with other like-minded people. Like professional and business lead organizations, these groups also require regular attendance and proactive involvement, which encourages relationship-building.

These service organizations are no doubt familiar to you. Rotary International, the oldest, limits its membership to owners, officers and partners in businesses. Kiwanis International, Lions Club and Optimist Club are open to all businesspeople.

But, be forewarned! You, as a woman, may not receive a warm welcome in some places. Depending upon the organization and the particular chapter you approach, women may not be allowed. It wasn't until the past decade that most of these organizations began admitting women. And still, although Rotary and Kiwanis declare that each chapter is free to decide whether to admit women, none are forced to.

Despite these remnants of exclusivity, women have made a big dent in the membership numbers in the past few years. Currently, Kiwanis International reports that in the six years since membership was opened to women, they've grown to approximately 25 percent of its membership. In some communities, women make up more than 75 percent of a chapter's membership.

If you're interested in joining a service organization, check the resources section in this book for headquarters addresses and phone numbers. You can contact them to find out if your local chapter allows women, or you can contact your local chamber of commerce to find out what's available in your area.

Women's organizations: Are they better?

Not only is there a National Association of Accountants, but there's an American Society of *Women* Accountants. In addition to the National Association of the Self-Employed, there are dozens of organizations for women business owners.

Do these organizations offer something that "co-ed" groups don't? Absolutely. But are they superior to such groups? Not necessarily.

Women's groups, profession-focused or general in nature, typically target topics and issues of special concern to women. For example, the National Association of Women in Construction is concerned with equitable representation in the profession, encouraging more women to enter this area, and providing scholarship programs. Another women's organization, the National Federation of Business and Professional Women, Inc., supports legislation that helps working women, and it encourages equity and economic self-sufficiency for all women.

Women's groups tend to focus their efforts on issues such as equal pay for equal work, fair advancement opportunities for women, hiring discrimination, workplace flexibility and childcare concerns.

There are numerous professional women's groups on a national level, which can be discovered in the *Encyclopedia of Associations*. Most have local chapters throughout the country, which offer regular luncheons, meetings and events. (Incidentally, membership in almost all of these organizations is *not* restricted to women.)

But there are plenty of women's organizations at the local and regional levels as well. These groups offer the advantage of addressing issues close to home. The Network of Women in Business, an Indianapolis-based group, has identified a primary mission as promoting women for placement on corporate and nonprofit boards of directors in the city. In addition, this group supports a job bank and an incubator for women (for more on incubators, see Chapter 15). Monthly meetings are supplemented by a number of informal networking groups scheduled for different interests, such as "working moms," "entrepreneurship group" and "sales pros."

There's no reason to believe that women's groups are superior—or inferior for that matter—in terms of networking effectiveness. But such a group is certainly more likely to address "women's issues" in more depth. And for those who still may be uncomfortable with the idea of professional hobnobbing, joining a women's group may seem more familiar. Kim Hackett, president of the Women's Home Business Network (WHBN), which is currently extending its reach beyond Indiana, comments, "A lot of women may be intimidated by an aggressive networking atmosphere. They don't like the idea of having to turn into men in order to do business. We provide a very informal, familiar environment."

The online you

Let's face it. Whether we like it or not, computer communication is a presence that can't be ignored. And while experts argue how pervasive—and even effective—the Information Highway is and will continue to be in our work and personal lives, there's no arguing that computers can offer us additional opportunities to network with those who share our interests.

46

Despite having spent the last eight years or so doing virtually all my professional work on a personal computer, I remain in virtual stupidity when it comes to understanding the Internet and the miracles of computer communication. Not only do I not know how to get on the Information Highway, I'm convinced that once there, I'd get lost and end up roaming its backroads for all cyber-eternity.

Nevertheless, through my CompuServe membership, I'm slowly edging my way onto that ever-widening road, timidly exploring some of the opportunities for networking. I correspond with a growing list of CompuServe members via e-mail. And I also check into various forums and conferences from time to time.

But my greatest online accomplishment was being interviewed on Women's Wire, another online service, for a book I'd written. While a moderator facilitated the interview, other members joined the interview, asking questions, sharing experiences and offering their own viewpoints. And, if I do say so myself, I came off quite eloquently—my responses seeming much more confident without the usual "uhs," "umms" and "ya knows" that so frequently blemish my radio interviews.

—B

Some of the best opportunities for sticking a toe into the ocean of computer communication—even if you're not yet ready to surf its waves—is to join a commercial online service such as America Online, CompuServe or PRODIGY. Once the software is installed, you typically pay a monthly fee for basic services (CompuServe's is $9.95 or thereabouts), plus online time for other services. These services provide easy-to-understand menus for introduction into forums, live talk and even the Internet.

For example, under CompuServe's Professional Forums, you can pick up information and drop in on correspondence regarding a number of topics. There's a Computer Consultants forum, an Entrepreneur's Small Business forum, a Court Reporters forum, a Journalism forum, a PR and Marketing forum, even a Rotarians Online forum.

The Entrepreneur's Small Business forum, for example, features a number of topics for investigation—such as "Business Start-up," "Legal Concerns," "Home-based Business" and "The Water Cooler."

It is possible to even job-hunt online—in the forums, there are often individuals seeking professional expertise for everything from how-to authors to seminar planners. There's a classifieds forum, listing "want ads" for a variety of professions. In addition, there are a number of online job-hunting services, which connect job-seekers to employers. Such services include Job Bank USA, kiNexus and Connexion. Several are listed in the resources section of this book, along with details about some of the commercial online services mentioned here.

Perhaps, though, the greatest value of networking in cyberspace is just sharing experiences and information. New business startups can learn from others how they've dealt with tax issues, workers can seek advice on salary negotiation, writers can ask other writers about fair royalty arrangements.

One online service that may be of particular interest is Women's Wire, the nation's only commercial online service focused on women. Launched in January 1994, the service currently has more than 1,500 subscribers. Women's Wire provides information about topics of interest to women, from spousal abuse to women's health issues to job and career concerns. Members can communicate via e-mail, open forums, private chats and scheduled conferences. In a recent newspaper interview (*San Francisco Sunday Examiner and Chronicle*), co-owner and co-founder Ellen Pack reported, "We've actually helped women find jobs, get better jobs and negotiate better salaries. One woman talked to our career coach online and was able to negotiate a better salary and a permanent position."

Conclusion

I read somewhere that everybody on this planet is separated by only six other people...six degrees of separation between the president of the United States and a gondolier in Venice, just filll in the names. You have to find the right six people. It's a profound thought: Everybody is near a door opening into other worlds.

—From "Six Degrees of Separation"

In this chapter, we've introduced a variety of sources for networking contacts, but the list is by no means exhaustive. Essentially, wherever and whenever people gather, there is networking potential—in the airport lounge, with the UPS person, waiting in line at the bank. And whether we're really only six people away from everyone else on the planet as the quote from the play *Six Degrees of Separation* suggests, by broadening our outlook and seeking out opportunities to connect with a wider range of people, we truly can make our world a little smaller.

Chapter 4

Networking roles: Mentor, matchmaker or supporter?

Within your network, you're bound to come across all sorts of helpful characters—from cheerleaders, coaches and fans to advice-givers, anchors, role models and experts. Depending upon each person's particular strengths, experiences and unique communication style, you'll interact and help one another in different ways. You'll turn to one person for encouragement and another for a no holds-barred critique. You'll ask for information from some and others will come to you. You may get together weekly to share experiences and support with your closest contacts, while touching base only occasionally with other connections, perhaps to exchange leads or seek advice.

There are as many networking styles in the world as there are networking individuals, but the key roles a networker may play can be narrowed down to three: The matchmaker, the mentor and the supporter.

Matchmakers: the people-connectors

Matchmakers tend to be sociable creatures, seeking out not only group functions, but actively pursuing one-on-one connections as well. Matchmakers, like all good networkers, draw on the arsenal of characteristics listed in Chapter 3 to strengthen their connections. They're curious about others, expressing genuine interest in the goals and activities of those they meet. They listen well and will prod others to talk about themselves.

Matchmakers don't stop at the question, "So, what do you do?" or "Who do you work for?" They will follow up with responses such as, "Tell me more about how you got involved with sports reporting," or "You must be a very determined woman to have made it so far in a male-dominated field." Bottom line, their reactions communicate that they're interested.

But it's what these individuals do with the details they learn from you and others that really sets them apart as matchmakers. *They make connections.* You tell Toni about your newfound interest in country dancing, but can't find anyone to go to the cowboy bar with you. She remembers Dolores, a woman from her office, talking about the two-step lessons she's been taking. She puts you in touch. Result? A match.

Women, particularly, are strong at this aspect of networking. "Who are the matchmakers of the world?" points out networking instructor Alice Ostrower. "Who has traditionally had to find the carpools and help kids find new playmates when they move to a new area? We really do have a natural ability to network. It's almost a maternal instinct."

Indeed, it is this ability to make connections that made the old-country matchmakers so indispensable. They could see marriage possibilities where other people were blind to them. (Remember Yenta the matchmaker from *Fiddler on the Roof*? When she suggests the betrothal of a nearsighted girl to a homely young man, she reasons, "With his looks and her eyes, it's a perfect match!")

An automatic connection

Kathy Dailey is a communications specialist and training consultant in the Midwest whose friends and business associates would identify one of her networking strengths as her ability to put people together. She says matchmaking is something she just can't help doing. "When I hear someone talking about a problem or a project, I automatically make connections and say, 'Oh, you should talk to so-and-so about that.' " She continues, "It only makes sense to tap into the skills, experiences and contacts of others, because we can't do it all and know it all ourselves. The next best thing is to know where to find the expertise or connections."

Dailey finds herself frequently riffling through her Rolodex, to put a graphic designer in touch with a newsletter editor, to give a phone number of a freelance writer to a friend in the publishing business or to pass on the name of her plumber to a neighbor.

Matchmakers like Dailey tend to blur the lines between their personal and business lives. "You never know where you'll find a match," she says. And indeed good matchmakers jump back and forth, perhaps giving their accountant some names of business card designers, putting a boss in touch with a friend who's a caterer, giving a client the name of a good divorce lawyer.

These individuals aren't always matching people with *people*. They're able to make other connections as well. They frequently know where to find information such as salary ranges, which industry publications offer the best inside track on job opportunities or which professional associations offer the most value.

Matchmakers are readily found in all categories of contacts, from family to professional groups. And these individuals will prove to be valuable networking contacts, no matter where you are in your career cycle—starting out, looking for a job, advancing your career, going out on your own. You can always use a good matchmaker to put you in touch with others who can provide job leads, information sources and expand your networking web.

When working with a matchmaker

1. Keep her informed about your activities. Because of her ability to see connections, she may think of courses of action or valuable contacts you wouldn't consider—or even ask for.

2. Keep her posted about progress in matches she's made. Let her know when you met with her contact and how it went.

3. *Always* treat her contacts with dignity and respect. A matchmaker's relationships are very valuable to her. Although she may be generous in sharing them with you, be careful not to abuse these introductions in any way. Don't make unrealistic time demands, for example, or push a new contact to give you a job, a lead or information if he or she isn't comfortable in doing so. Word of rude or unprofessional behavior will get back to your matchmaker, and could do serious damage to your relationship.

4. Don't forget to thank her. Your matchmaking contact may work at such lightning speed and with such smoothness you may not even recognize her efforts.

5. Provide honest feedback regarding the value of her matches. If, for example, you had a bad experience with a vendor she referred to you, it'll be important to her to know this. A matchmaker banks her reputation on the strength of her contacts.

6. Do some matchmaking for *her* from time to time. Even if it's not an introduction that brings a job, an important contact, business, etc., she'll still appreciate the effort. And she always values opportunities to grow her network.

When acting as a matchmaker

1. Listen for opportunities to make connections. Often your networking contacts won't directly ask for a referral. But if you see an opportunity to introduce two people who might benefit from such a meeting, go for it. A good matchmaker is *never* proprietary about her contacts when a match could prove beneficial to both parties!

2. Protect your contacts from abuse or wasted time. Don't give out names to known pests or "takers." Don't give out names of individuals you know are terribly busy or currently unavailable. And don't refer your contacts to people who are known to be rude or who don't return phone calls.

3. When in doubt, ask a contact if you can pass on his or her name to someone else. Don't assume!

4. Warn individuals when you've passed on their name. Give them the name of the individual who will be contacting them, so that when they receive the call, they will readily make the connection.

5. Be careful to "pace" your matchmaking efforts so you're not loading up one individual with too many referrals.

Mentors: updating a traditional role

Traditionally, mentoring has involved the pairing up of a promising young employee with a higher-placed, more experienced individual within the same company. The mentor spends a significant amount of time providing guidance and support and nurturing the talents of the novice. Traditionally, this relationship would often last the lifetime of a career. Most often, mentoring is carried out on an informal basis, although some companies do provide structured mentoring programs. (Hewlett-Packard's Leadership Effectiveness and Development Program and J.C. Penney Company's "Buddy System," for example. Read more about such programs in Chapter 11.)

Indeed, mentoring has been a good-old-boy tradition, one in which women played little part. Why? Because mentors tend to nurture relationships with people similar to themselves. With few women in the executive ranks, even fewer women were able to take advantage of mentor relationships. Additionally, because of attitudes and issues regarding age and gender in the work place, it's been rare for older, higher-ranked males to foster younger, less-experienced females. A male executive may be reluctant to advertise support for female staff for fear that others would assume their relationship was sexual. Or he may worry about the potential for harassment issues. And a woman risks resentment from others who might assume she's trying to "sleep her way to the top."

Modernizing a good-old-boy tradition

But mentoring in the business world is changing—which opens up more opportunities for women. Today, with the breakdown of the traditional hierarchical management structure, there is less of a tendency to turn to next-in-line superiors within the company for mentoring guidance. We seek mentors from outside our own work environment, perhaps turning to a former boss who now works for a competitor or associated industry. Mentors may come from professional groups, or former vendor or client relationships. If you're in your own business, you will probably turn to other small-business owners, those who may have been in business longer or have had greater success, to provide mentorship guidance.

Also, in a climate where few people stay with the same company throughout their career, it's more likely (and more advantageous according to many) for individuals to have a number of mentors at any given time.

Author Susan RoAne eschews what she terms "mentor monogamy" and encourages networkers to seek out MOMs, "mentors of the moment." In her book, *The Secrets of Savvy Networking,* she explains, "Mobility, career changes and 'downsizing' have wreaked havoc on the 'safe-haven-for-30-years-until-I-get-the-gold-watch' syndrome. Consequently, the single-mentor theory is as full of holes as the single-bullet theory in the JFK assassination. We need to expand our thinking."

How to hook up with strong mentors

Linda Phillips-Jones, psychologist and author of *The New Mentors and Protégés,* encourages us to go beyond our own immediate workplace. In a speech she gave to the Sixth National Association for Female Executives (NAFE) Satellite Conference, she advised attendees to think of every successful person as a possible mentor, starting with their current boss ("Even if you think this person is more of a *tor*mentor..."). Once you identify the kinds of help you require, write the names of all individuals who seem very competent in these areas. In addition, she advises, consider how you might be of value to your potential mentor.

Phillips-Jones advises preparing to approach a mentor candidate the same way you'd prepare for a job interview: "Find out all you can about the individual's work, special interests, needs and interaction style." Just as you'd prepare for an interview by learning as much as you could about the company and the person hiring, it will be to your advantage to be as familiar as possible with your prospective mentor.

However, your candidate for mentor should be familiar with you *before* you request from him or her commitment to a mentor relationship. Don't expect someone to invest in you if he or she hasn't been exposed to your work or knows you in some way.

You might approach your candidate by asking for a short meeting—in the workplace or even a lunch meeting. Be clear and specific about what your intentions are: "I've discovered that you are the kind of professional I aspire to be. I'd like to be able to meet with you, once a month for no longer than an hour—if that would be convenient for you—just to get your specific advice on goals and some of the important issues and challenges I'm facing."

Once you gain commitment from your mentor, assume responsibility for keeping the connection—at least initially. Set up meetings and keep them brief, as promised. Keep to an agenda and offer follow-up reports on issues discussed in previous meetings. While this may seem a little *too* structured at first, your relationship will undoubtedly loosen up into something more comfortable for both you and your mentor—something that will offer much more give-and-take.

Fundamentally, a mentor is a source of expertise and knowledge that you don't yet have. Yet he or she can serve as a matchmaker or a supporter as well. A mentor in your company may smooth the way for your promotion. A mentor in your professional organization may introduce you to important contacts who might provide you with job or business opportunities. He or she may recommend valuable vendors or professionals such as accountants or attorneys. Your mentor may teach you how to use the new software on your computer—or simply inspire you when you feel discouraged.

When it's no longer working

Because your circumstances may change—new employer, new career, new technology—you may discover your mentor is no longer able to effectively serve in that capacity. You may have outgrown him or her. You may even discover that your mentor is actually uncomfortable with your success, begrudging the fact that you may have surpassed him or her in expertise or recognition. If you find yourself in one of these situations, it's time to move on. Typically, these types of situations take care of themselves, and the two of you will just drift apart. But it may be necessary for you to proactively break off the connection. It's best to be honest: "I feel I've grown to a point where I'm not utilizing your time fairly. I'd like to keep in contact with you, but maybe as a colleague instead."

When working with a mentor

1. Don't take your mentor for granted. Be sure to acknowledge your mentor's contributions with thank-you notes, lunches and other forms of appreciation.

2. It may seem perfectly natural to let mentor relationships develop into one-sided affairs. After all, the mentor has all the experience, so it's easy to let him or her do all the giving. But even if you are not your mentor's equal in experience, skill or connections, you still have plenty to offer. You undoubtedly will be able to share connections, information and experiences as well.

3. Respect your mentor's time. Be prepared with specific topics, questions or problems when you meet.

4. Be willing to accept your mentor's input, even criticism. And be prepared to act on your mentor's advice.

When acting as a mentor

1. In order to be a good mentor, you must be willing to make a commitment. Mentoring doesn't mean tossing off advice or bits of wisdom when it suits your schedule. Be prepared to invest time and energy into the individual.

2. Listen! Because you're the mentor, you might fall into the trap of doing all the talking. Listening is always important when networking, but particularly in a mentoring situation. You're there to *guide* and *coach*, not lecture and pontificate.

3. Give constructive feedback. Offer specifics whenever possible. Instead of "You need to work on your negotiating skills," point to identifiable behaviors: "When you crossed your arms and pushed your chair away from the table, I saw the negotiations come to a halt. Keep your body language open."

4. Recognize when it's time to end the mentoring relationship. This could happen for a number of reasons: Your protégé has reached an experience level that surpasses yours, one of you can't commit the time or effort to maintain the relationship, or your mentee's goals have changed. Chances are, you'll know when it's time to say good-bye. There may be a distance or an awkwardness between you, or perhaps you don't make as much of an effort to get together. When it happens, look at it as a positive sign. You've fulfilled a need, and your protégé is now comfortable in pursuing his or her career goals without you. Offer your congratulations and suggest you continue on as colleagues.

Supporters: shared resources, information exchange

Lori Bennett, a marketing research and litigation consultant in the Midwest, gets together with former co-workers-turned-business-owners on a regular basis. "We talk about everything from office furniture to taxes to health insurance to working in our bathrobes," she says. "We're all pretty much in the same boat. Even though our businesses are different, we all started out at the same time and are running into similar problems. It's good to share experiences and even commiserate about the problems that befall us." She says that the members do share business leads, but the biggest value to her, she reports, is the sharing of knowledge, information and resources.

Bennett points to an experience with one member of the group, whose discussions over margaritas and salsa range from business matters to gossip about their former employer. "I was desperate to find a good health insurance plan. John had recently joined an entrepreneur's association that provided a plan as well as other benefits to the self-employed. I'd never have known about it if he hadn't told me."

The members of Bennett's informal networking group are serving each other as *supporters*. They listen, they share, they encourage and they cry on each others' shoulders if necessary. While members may offer each other referrals as well as mentorship assistance, the primary value of the group is the exchange of experiences and information.

Knowledge networks: source of supporters

A group who shares a profession makes for an excellent source of supporters, whether it's a loosely structured group that meets without an agenda or an international professional association. *Megatrends* author John Naisbitt refers to these groups as *knowledge networks*. They are valuable, Naisbitt says, because they work to "foster self-help, exchange information, change society, improve productivity and work life and share resources." While such relationships most often come from others in the same field, supporters can be found outside of professional groups and circles of colleagues.

In the corporate world, supporters may also come from the ranks of co-workers and former co-workers, even vendors and clients. For the self-employed, supporters can be drawn from others who are self-employed, whether or not they're in the same field. (As Bennett discovered, accountants, PR professionals and training consultants are as valuable to her as those in her own line of work.) In addition, vendors, as well as associates and former co-workers in the corporate world, can serve as supporters to the self-employed.

Computer-savvy individuals can find an additional source of supporters online. The multitude of bulletin boards and forums offer opportunities galore for requesting information, seeking advice or just sounding off. (For more detail on online networking, see Chapter 3.)

Finding supporters in women's groups

Women's professional groups provide an excellent source of supporters. Kim Hackett started the Women's Home Business Network (WHBN) in Indianapolis to gain support, ideas and advice from other women working from home. Today, WHBN is an incorporated, nonprofit organization with a membership of nearly 200. The organization plans to start other chapters nationwide.

"We're pretty much a support group," she explains. "We come together to learn and meet other entrepreneurs, to share frustrations and successes. What's different about us is that we get down to the nitty and the gritty." This "nitty and gritty" includes seminars and conferences on working at home, a bimonthly newsletter with profiles and tips for home-based businesses and speakers at the monthly meetings.

"We are filling a particular niche that other organizations aren't," says Hackett, who believes the group appeals to women because they've discovered its sensitivity to work issues that primarily challenge women, such as balancing work and family.

Sensitivity and empathy are indeed key trademarks of a good supporter or support group. Supporters, it should come as no surprise, can be expected to serve double-duty, functioning as matchmakers or mentors, serving as sounding boards, experts or critics when the situation requires it. Bennett, for example, may bring a newly designed promotional brochure for her business to a group get-together. She'll request feedback and get responses that may include a design modification from a graphic designer, the name of a reasonably priced printer from a consultant, a request for the name of her copywriter and perhaps an unqualified approval of the brochure.

Beware of some supporters

Supporters present different communication styles—and in all likelihood you'll enjoy the diversity of quiet assurers, tactful evaluators and enthusiastic encouragers. But there are some styles that you'll want to watch out for.

This one, for example: You may have identified someone in your networking circle as a supporter because he or she is always willing to commiserate with you. You didn't get the job you were hoping for? You can count on Ray to take you out for a beer and curse corporate America for rejecting you. But, can you count on him when the going is *good*? Would Ray have taken you out for a beer if you were celebrating a promotion? Was he there to build you up before you went for the job interview? Some individuals seem comfortable around you only when things are going badly. But when you have successes to celebrate, they're often missing.

Still, others may act to discourage your ideas and dreams. Gilda Carle, management consultant and president of Interchange Communications Training, called them "drainers," speaking at the Sixth National Association for Female Executives (NAFE) Satellite Conference in May 1995. "Are you kidding me? You're thinking about doing that?" are the types of comments heard from a drainer when you present your ideas or goals, she says. Drainers seem to be there to diminish your pleasure with remarks that squelch your enthusiasm. This type of person can sabotage your self-esteem and positive attitude.

Working with supporters

1. When identifying the best supporters from among your contacts, look for characteristics such as strong listening skills, willingness to share information, experiences and resources and empathy.
2. Typically, those individuals you share some career commonality with make for the best supporters—whether it's the same job, the same employer, the same industry or even the fact that you're both self-employed.
3. Be sensitive to the fair-exchange philosophy. Even when we're talking information, don't take without giving in return.

4. Work to keep the overall tone of your relationship upbeat. Sometimes there's a tendency for supporter relationships to be built on shared suffering. Whether it's commiserating over the tax burden among the self-employed or anticipating the next round of restructuring within a company, your interactions might easily slip into the cynical. Make sure you enjoy positive exchanges as well.

5. Supporter relationships, more so than mentor or matchmaker, tend to inspire sharing of confidences. Maintain a professional distance, however, in most situations. Don't reveal company or departmental secrets, or do or say anything that could compromise your professional integrity.

6. In professional groups that are informal or loosely structured, there may be a danger of losing focus on the "professional" goals of the group. Particularly when a group of supporters enjoys each other's company, the conversations may shift from business concerns to those of a personal nature. While socializing is an essential aspect of networking and even the most structured get-togethers couldn't hurt from a little small talk, keep the majority of the time spent on professional or career matters.

7. Know when to be critical. While everyone wants encouragement and positive reinforcement, there are times when it's important to hear the "bad news" as well. As a supporter, you owe it to your networking connections to provide honest feedback, even if it may include criticism. And you'll want to make sure that your supporter contacts are giving you the same.

Conclusion

In any given networking relationship, the roles we've described here are neither rigid nor exclusive. Your mentor, for example, can turn into your supporter. And a supporter can function as matchmaker when the occasion calls for it. You can serve as supporter for one colleague, act as mentor for another and be a matchmaker for both. But it's important to be able to identify these key roles you and your contacts may play, so that you can polish the requisite communication skills and serve as a better networker.

Part 2

Living the networking way of life

Chapter 5

Self-awareness: Setting the scene for networking success

I always wanted to be somebody, but I should have been more specific.
—Lily Tomlin and Jane Wagner

Know thyself—throughout history, the dictum has been addressed by poets, philosophers, shamans and shams. While this chapter isn't exactly about finding the path to enlightenment through self-awareness, it *is* about coming to understand specifics about yourself. It's about taking the time to acquaint yourself with your own needs and goals.

Why? Because as networking pro Alice Ostrower insists, self-awareness and acceptance is a key to effective networking. "Each person has to be comfortable with himself or herself first," she says. In order to enlist others to be of help to you, you have to be in a position to be able to communicate what it is you need. And in order to do that, *you* have to know who you are and what you want.

Sounds pretty elementary, maybe *too* simple. But it's surprising how little thought we give to issues of self-evaluation and goals, in all phases of our career. Having been in the position of hiring, we too often run into interviewees who can't answer questions such as "What makes you qualified for this position?" Or "What are your career goals?" These people—as Tomlin and Wagner mused—need to be more specific.

No matter where you are in your career lifecycle, it's absolutely essential that you know what you have to offer and what you want to do with it. So if you're in doubt, set aside the time—*now*—for a serious self-inventory session. Spend the amount of time it takes—whether an hour over coffee or a weekend-long retreat—to do some soul-searching. Take the steps you need to take, and get some good books for guidance. (*What Color Is Your Parachute?* by Richard Nelson Bolles and *Do What You Love, The Money Will Follow* by Marsha Sinetar are two books that offer some excellent self-inventory and goal-identification exercises.) Consult a career counselor if you must.

Goals: the power behind your career growth

Knowing what your personal strengths and career goals are will help you get more out of networking. Why? Because you'll be more effective at sharing your experiences and desires with your contacts in quantifiable ways. Think of it this way: How would you respond to a comment like this? "Gee, my job is so unfulfilling. I don't know how much longer I'll be able to stand it. But what else can I do?" You'd probably offer some sympathy, extend a pat on the shoulder and perhaps buy your friend a drink.

Now, consider this statement: "You know, I've concluded that I really am good at what I do. After all, I wouldn't keep breaking departmental goals if I weren't. But I really miss people contact and it's clear to me that I'd be much happier working directly with the clients rather than behind the scenes. Therefore, I'm going to explore two directions: Getting a promotion to account executive—or going out on my own. Do you know anyone who can give me advice?"

First of all, the second response is much more positive and action-oriented. This individual clearly has an understanding of her capabilities and has given thought to what would make her happy. And, secondly, because she understands this, she's able to give her networking contacts specific ways they can assist her. That makes her easier to help.

Your professional self: a work in progress

Just as today's work force is an ever-changing beast, your career status is never static, but always in a state of flux. Your goals and needs as a career ingenue are quite different than your priorities and desires at the peak of your career. The following is only a sampling of the types of career goals you could be considering:

- You may be looking for a new job.
- You may be entering the work force for the first time in years.
- You may be in a position to step away from your career for a while, and spend time on family and volunteer activities.
- You may want to change careers completely.
- You may want to broaden your skills or go back to school.
- You may want to work on your own.
- You may want to be back in the corporate fold, after a stint in your own business.

Whatever your personal goals are, it's important that you stay in touch with them, so that you can recognize and respond to opportunities that cross your path, and share your goals and dreams with those of your networking contacts who may be in a position to help you along the way.

As we said in Chapter 1, change is the byword in today's career lifecycle. That's okay. It's just important that you stay on top of that change, updating your skills inventory and your career goals on a regular basis.

Some self-assessment exercises

We've included a few worksheets to get those thinking processes started. (They'll make great reference material for resume preparation, as well!) The first worksheets capture your work or volunteer experiences. Make as many copies as you need to record all your work and volunteer experiences. Following these are worksheets on education and training information.

The skills summary worksheet, though it may require some thought, will prove particularly valuable. It will be helpful to read back through your other worksheets to get a sense of what your key skills are. But go beyond the rigid structure of job titles and degrees. Yes, as an accountant, you may have a way with numbers. But you may also win points with your boss because of your artfully crafted memos to the company, or your ability to settle inter-departmental disputes over budget problems.

Do some careful exploration to come up with the skills you may have demonstrated above and beyond your job description. Also, consider hobbies (photography, sports coaching) or skills you may not be called upon to use in your job (fluency in a foreign language). Here is a list to get you started:

Leadership	Communication	Customer service
Public speaking	Marketing	Sales
Negotiation	Motivational	Marketing
Attention to detail	Computer skills	Networking
Follow-up	Language	Teaching or training
Coaching	Creative thinking	Design
Interpersonal	Analytical	Self-motivated
Team playing	Organizational	Planning
Foreign language	Accounting	Interviewing
Listening	Management	Mechanical

Finally, we've included a worksheet that will stimulate your thinking about goals and career dreams as well. Please note, it's just a jumping-off point. True self-evaluation and goal-setting cannot be resolved by filling out a worksheet. It requires thoughtful exploration and soul-searching.

Conclusion

As the great American pianist, composer and wit Oscar Levant once said "It's not what you are, it's what you don't become that hurts." There's really nothing to fear from knowing yourself and identifying your needs and goals. At the same time, there's plenty to lose by failing to reach your potential—including your self-esteem and potential for success.

Networking can be powerful tool in your quest for career success, but you'll have to know yourself to have well-developed relationships with others. The process doesn't have to be complicated or difficult—and if you find there are things you don't like so well, make a note, because this is your opportunity to make changes. So if you haven't already done so, *now's* the time to meet the most important person in your network—*yourself.*

Work experience

Make one copy of this worksheet for each paid job or professional internship position you have held.

1. Name of company_____

2. Address and phone number_____
_____
_____

3. Your job title (use the actual title that would be on employee records)_____
_____

4. Start and end dates (month and year)_____
_____

5. Salary (beginning and end)_____

6. Supervisor's name and title_____

7. General job description (one or two sentence summary of your job)_____
_____
_____
_____

8. Responsibilities

   Management/supervisory duties (include size of staff and specific duties—hiring, training, etc.)_____
_____
_____
_____
_____

   Budgetary/financial duties (include any duties related to money—writing a budget, totaling daily receipts, analyzing cost/profit ratios, etc.)_____
_____
_____
_____

   Sales/marketing duties (include specifics about product sold, type of customer base, advertising responsibilities, long-term marketing planning, etc.)_____
_____
_____
_____
_____

Customer service (include number of customers you served on a regular basis, plus their status—retail customers, executive-level clients, etc.)_____

_____

_____

_____

_____

Production duties (include amount of goods/services produced on a daily, monthly or annual basis)_____

_____

_____

_____

_____

Technical duties (any duties that required you to use computers or other technical equipment)_____

_____

_____

_____

_____

_____

9. Accomplishments (including honors and awards)_____

_____

_____

_____

_____

_____

_____

10. Special skills learned (computer skills, telephone sales, desktop publishing, etc.)_____

_____

_____

_____

_____

_____

_____

Volunteer experience

Make one copy of this worksheet for each volunteer activity.

1. Name of organization_____

2. Address and phone number_____

_____

3. Position/title (if no position held, simply indicate "member")_____

_____

4. Start and end dates of this position_____

5. Start and end dates of your membership (month and year)_____

6. Hours devoted per week_____

7. Name(s) of organization president(s) or your ranking superior_____

_____

8. General description (one or two sentence summary of your job)_____

_____

_____

_____

9. Responsibilities

    Management/supervisory duties (include size of staff and specific duties—coordinating, training, etc.)_____

_____

_____

_____

_____

    Budgetary/financial duties (include any duties related to money—writing a budget, totaling sales receipts, analyzing cost/profit ratios, etc.)_____

_____

_____

_____

_____

    Sales/marketing duties (include specifics about product sold, type of customer base, advertising responsibilities, long-term marketing planning, etc.)___

_____

_____

_____

_____

_____

Customer service (include number of "customers" you contacted on a regular basis, plus their status—high-school students, disabled adults, community leaders, etc.)_____

_____

_____

_____

_____

_____

Production duties (include amount of goods/services produced on a daily, monthly or annual basis)_____

_____

_____

_____

Technical duties (any duties that required you to use computers or other technical equipment)_____

_____

_____

_____

_____

_____

10. Accomplishments (including honors and awards)_____

_____

_____

_____

_____

_____

11. Special skills learned (computer skills, telephone sales, desktop publishing, etc.)_____

_____

_____

_____

_____

_____

_____

_____

Education

High school education

(If you have many years of experience under your belt, you need only complete questions 1-6 for high school education.)

1. School name_____
2. Address (city and state)_____
_____
3. Years attended_____
4. Year graduated_____
5. GPA/class rank_____
6. Honors (valedictorian, top 10%, scholarship recipient, etc.)_____
_____
7. Accomplishments_____
_____
8. Major courses_____
_____
9. Special skills learned_____
_____

Post-secondary education

(List college, trade school and postgraduate work.)

1. School name_____
2. Address (city and state)_____
_____
3. Years attended_____
4. Year graduated_____
5. GPA/class rank_____
6. Honors (valedictorian, top 10%, scholarship recipient, etc.)_____
_____
7. Accomplishments_____
_____
8. Major courses_____
_____
9. Special skills learned_____
_____
_____

Post-secondary education

1. School name_____

2. Address (city and state)_____

_____

3. Years attended_____

4. Year graduated_____

5. GPA/class rank_____

6. Honors (valedictorian, top 10%, scholarship recipient, etc.)_____

_____

7. Accomplishments_____

_____

8. Major courses_____

_____

_____

9. Special skills learned_____

_____

_____

Post-secondary education

1. School name_____

2. Address (city and state)_____

_____

3. Years attended_____

4. Year graduated_____

5. GPA/class rank_____

6. Honors (valedictorian, top 10%, scholarship recipient, etc.)_____

_____

7. Accomplishments_____

_____

8. Major courses_____

_____

_____

9. Special skills learned_____

_____

_____

Other training

1. Training received/license or certification earned_____

_____

2. Name of training institution_____
3. Address and phone number_____

_____

4. Start and end dates of training_____
5. Name and title of instructor_____
6. Skills learned_____

_____

7. Accomplishments_____

_____

1. Training received/license or certification earned_____

_____

2. Name of training institution_____
3. Address and phone number_____

_____

4. Start and end dates of training_____
5. Name and title of instructor_____
6. Skills learned_____

_____

7. Accomplishments_____

_____

1. Training received/license or certification earned_____

_____

2. Name of training institution_____
3. Address and phone number_____

_____

4. Start and end dates of training_____
5. Name and title of instructor_____
6. Skills learned_____

_____

7. Accomplishments_____

_____

Skills summary

Skill area_____

Years experience in this area_____
Special training_____
_____
_____
_____
_____
_____

Accomplishments_____
_____
_____
_____
_____
_____
_____

Skill area_____

Years experience in this area_____
Special training_____
_____
_____
_____
_____
_____

Accomplishments_____
_____
_____
_____
_____
_____
_____

Skill area_____

Years experience in this area_____
Special training_____
_____
_____
_____
_____

Accomplishments_____
_____
_____
_____
_____
_____
_____

Skill area_____

Years experience in this area_____
Special training_____
_____
_____
_____
_____

Accomplishments_____
_____
_____
_____
_____
_____
_____

Goal identification worksheet

1. Identify the special talent or skill you most enjoy employing. (This doesn't have to be work-related. If you like to cook, for example, and could imagine a career that would involve cooking, catering, writing about food, or selling it, put it down.)

_____

_____

_____

_____

_____

What to do if you're stuck on this question: Ask yourself the following, and your answers should give you some clues:

What sort of activities did you love as a child?

_____

_____

_____

What do you like most about your current job?

_____

_____

_____

What do you do in your spare time?

_____

_____

_____

What do others compliment you for?

_____

_____

_____

2. List other special talents or skills you may have.

_____

_____

_____

3. Identify your long-term career goal, if known. (There's no need to be practical here. Let your imagination go: Want to write articles about the pyramids for *National Geographic?* Own your own peanut-butter-and-jelly sandwich restaurant? Write the Great American Novel?)

_____

_____

_____

_____

_____

_____

It's surprisingly easy to get stuck on this question. The world may be your oyster, but it's sometimes difficult to know exactly where to dive in order to find that special pearl—a fulfilling career. If you are struggling to come up with an answer, consider these questions to shake up some thoughts:

As a child, what did you want to be when you grew up?

_____

_____

_____

Whom do you admire? Who are your role models? (Consider acquaintances as well as celebrities or historical figures.)

_____

_____

_____

If you were going back to your high school reunion, what would you like to be able to tell people about yourself?

_____

_____

_____

If you were to be featured in *People* magazine, what would you like the article to be about?

_____

_____

_____

4. Do your special talents and your long-term career goal jibe (your skills are writing and creativity, and your goal is to write a science fiction novel, you're a great cook and you want to start a catering service)? If not, is there a way you can make a connection (you have great organizational and attention-to-detail skills and love to travel—a career in the travel industry might be for you)?

_____

_____

_____

_____

5. Identify the skills or training you may need to attain in order to achieve your long-term goal.

_____

_____

_____

_____

6. Identify what additional career steps you may need to take in order to attain your goal. (You want to open a coffee shop to rival Starbucks? Putting in some hours behind an espresso machine might be a necessary step.)

_____

_____

_____

_____

7. Identify who you know or who you'd like to know who might be able to offer you advice, experience or direction in attaining your goals.

_____

_____

_____

_____

_____

_____

Chapter 6

Identifying and evaluating your core network

In the business world, we've come to rely on the structures of the work environment. We turn to our Day-timers and Rolodexes, if not to our administrative assistants, to keep us organized and on schedule. We enter a meeting armed with an agenda and leave on a business trip with itinerary in hand. We approach our responsibilities and annual goals with business plans and proposals. Year-end reports and employee reviews tell us how we're doing.

While it may seem that we've become dependent upon these tools, they clearly make us more effective. Likewise, structure can help make our networking efforts more effective, particularly when we're starting out or if we're not quite at ease with the concept.

And there's nothing wrong with that. Structure is the harness that channels creative power in a productive direction. Becoming good at anything—whether it's ballet or brain surgery—requires practice, discipline and homework before it becomes "natural." Networking pro Alice Ostrower observes that although networking eventually becomes so natural you'll do it wherever you go, "it is a skill that has to be learned and has to be practiced."

Learning and practicing networking may involve the use of tools such as index cards, computer programs or daily planners. It might require role-playing with friends before you attend a function with networking potential. It may mean rehearsing dialogue before you call a referral, or keeping track of your contacts by means of a calendar or notebook. It will undoubtedly require some ongoing review, planning and evaluation on your part.

All this structure and effort may feel uncomfortable at first, perhaps even a little bit like acting. But as you become more practiced at networking, your activities will feel more natural, as if you were born to network.

So let's get started by putting some structure into the learning process: Identifying and evaluating your existing network of contacts. (An additional benefit of this exercise: You'll more than likely discover that you have a more extensive network than you may have imagined. Result? More confidence in working it and expanding it.)

We'll develop your network's structure by looking separately at your contacts with people and your involvement with professional and community organizations. We've provided worksheets to help you secure the information as well as sample worksheets with hypothetical information as examples.

But just as we stressed in Chapter 5, the important thing is to know where you stand with your network and to identify your goals for those relationships. The process outlined in this chapter will help you get there, but you can achieve the same result developing your own method.

Before you begin this process, you'll probably want to gather paper, pens and pencils. You'll be looking at all your current and potential contacts, and evaluating their networking potential. You may want to begin this process by making rough notes on paper, later transferring the data to the finished forms on pages 86 and 87. Or, you may want to duplicate the forms and use them to analyze all your contacts. You could also invent your own system. Read through the steps of the process, then get started using whatever method works best for you. What you need to do—no matter what system you use—is to gather all the information in one place, and organize it in such a way that you can easily review, evaluate and update it.

Identify the individuals in your network

1. Make a list. Refer back to Chapter 3 to help get you started identifying the individuals in your existing network. Write one list that includes all your *personal, community* and *professional* contacts. Think about this carefully and make sure you consider everyone, from your brother to your boss, including those who have the *potential* for becoming good contacts. Pore through your telephone/address book. Flip through your Rolodex. Review your holiday card list. Here's a list of possibilities to get you started:

Personal contacts

family members
friends and acquaintances
neighbors
former classmates (or current
    classmates if you're in school)
doctors
dentist

hair stylist
parents of children's friends
friends from the fitness center
accountant
insurance agent
real estate agent
lawyer

mechanic
therapist
nurses
landlord
banker
financial planner
UPS courier
waiter or bartender
children's teachers
teachers at adult classes
manicurist
personal trainer
masseuse
members of church or synagogue
members of PTA
youth sports coaches or parents
scout leaders or parents
members of sports teams
contacts from volunteer
   organizations
friends from alumni associations

contacts at fund raising
   organizations
members/staff of community
   centers
members of cultural organizations (art league, jazz society)
co-workers
former co-workers
bosses
former bosses
clients
former clients
vendors or suppliers
former vendors or suppliers
competitors
colleagues in professional
   groups
colleagues in service
   organizations
members of leads groups
friends and relatives of friends
   and relatives

2. Identify the networking connection. Now review your list, adding information about how you know the individuals as well as why you consider them networking contacts. This may include reasons that are not related to your business or profession. Here are a few examples:

Ted Simon: Neighbor. Owns a small PR business. His clients are mostly small to medium-sized businesses. He's active in Big Brothers. (Knows everything about lawn care!)

Regina King: Former co-worker. She's now marketing director in another company, and currently on the board of the local marketing association. Well-connected with the marketing community.

Les Norris: PTA parent. CPA. Member of local networking group I'm interested in joining.

Marty Kappelman: Director of neighborhood community center. Lots of community contacts through her fund-raising activities. We share the same musical interests—she sings at the local piano bar!

3. Identify *their* connections. If possible, identify who your contacts may know. For instance, among Ted's PR clients (see the preceding examples) are some companies that might offer business opportunities for you. Same with Regina and Marty. Write down the names of your *contact's* contacts, and any details you know about their relationship with your contact. Under Marty, for example:

Johnson Dean Inc: A large advertising firm that contributes to the community center. Marty is good friends with Scott Dean, who often provides his services to the center's promotional efforts.

4. Outline your networking history. For each individual you've identified, list any networking activity you may have had in the past. Did one of you introduce the other to potential networking connections? Provide a lead on work or jobs? Professional information? Here's an example for Regina King:

Known her for eight years, worked together for five years. She's put me in touch with four members of her marketing association; three introductions led to business for me. She also passes on assignments to me from time to time. I referred a job candidate to her, whom she eventually hired. I give her feedback on her direct-mail pieces occasionally. We meet at least once a month.

5. Qualify the relationship. To the degree that you can, characterize your level of interaction with each contact. Do you have a strong, long-term friendship? A long-term but strictly professional relationship? Is this a casual, occasional contact?

Ted: Casual. Talk occasionally when we pick up our morning papers at the same time.

Regina: Strong. Good friend as well as long-term colleague.

This is an important step because it will help you with the *next* step, which is to identify which relationships you'd like to cultivate.

6. Identify your goal for this relationship. Perhaps you've classified a few of your networking relationships as strong—these are individuals you feel you could tap for any number of needs. Great. You have a good solid foundation supporting your network, and in future chapters, you'll learn more about maintaining and strengthening these relationships.

But in the process, you've undoubtedly identified other relationships that might not be where you want them. Perhaps there's an individual you feel you've "hit it off" with, and you suspect could develop into a fulfilling relationship; maybe there's an acquaintance who seems to know everybody; or even a former employer you believe has mentor potential.

It's important to pinpoint these relationships because they offer potential for expanding your network. Identify these individuals and think about how you'd like the relationship to grow. And don't just consider what your contact can do for *you*, but also how you can be of value to that person. For example:

Les: He's expressed a desire to promote his business in the community. I could help him with this. I could also give him business leads. I'd like to join his networking group—maybe he could sponsor me. He could also refer business to me.

7. Identify your core network. If you've completed the previous steps in this exercise, you have probably already identified your core network. By listing and evaluating each of your connections, it should become clear that there are some individuals you have a lot more interaction with than others.

According to Melissa Giovagnoli, author of *Make Your Connections Count,* a manageable "primary" (or core) network is made up of about 10 people or less. These are people who complement who you are and what you do. Perhaps your core network includes contacts with a variety of viewpoints and expertise, or perhaps the network is somewhat redundant—with most of the contacts coming from among your family, personal friends or co-workers.

At this point, it's as much a matter of quantity as it is one of quality; you need to see how big your core network is and who's in it. Even if most of your primary contacts are family members or lifelong friends, there's plenty of power wherever two people put their heads together. Later on, you may need to expand or change the makeup of your core network. But don't worry, you don't have to give up your friends and family to do it. It will simply grow and change over time, as a result of setting and achieving your goals.

In later chapters we'll talk about the ways in which you can explore, develop, expand and change your core network and networking relationships.

Identify your community and professional affiliations

Now we turn our attention from people to *groups* of people. Think about all the groups you belong to (you've probably already listed some of the individuals in these groups in your list of networking contacts). Consider service organizations, professional organizations and women's groups, your church or synagogue, classes you're taking at a community college, even your membership at a fitness center, especially if you take a class. Don't forget the PTA and any kids' activities that you're involved in, from sports to scouts. Here are some examples to get your thinking process started:

Community and professional contacts

church or synagogue
PTA
youth sports teams
youth scouts
adult sports teams
community classes
volunteer organizations
alumni associations
YMCA or other community
   centers
homeowner associations
neighborhood watch groups
cultural organizations (art
   league, jazz society)
fund raising organizations

YMCA or other community
   centers
political groups
Toastmasters
Industry associations (such as
   American Marketing Assn.,
   etc.)
Business referral groups
Kiwanis International
Lions Club
Rotary International
Optimists
Your employer (if self-
   employed, your business)

Identify the number and types of individuals in the group. Indicate how many contact opportunities you have, and describe the organization and its membership. For example:

Neighborhood association: Approximately 30 families. A lot of retired business people, several who are still members of professional groups. Couples in 30s and 40s, dual-income families mostly.

Camp committee at the community center: 7 women, 4 men. All parents with kids in 5 to 12 range. Range from stay-at-home parents to professionals (2 doctors, 2 lawyers).

Evaluate the networking potential of this group. Based on factors like size, makeup of membership and contact opportunities, determine how much networking potential the group carries. While virtually any activity holds opportunities for networking, some activities offer more than others. And when it comes to prioritizing your commitments, or choosing between them, it's important to know which bring you the most value.

Do you see this group offering opportunities for matchmaking contacts and business leads? Or will it more likely serve as a knowledge network? Is it a small group that is conducive to relationship-building? Does it offer opportunities to get involved—workshops, special events, community programs? Determine how the group can better serve your networking needs.

Identify your networking goals for this group. Long-term, you may determine that you hope to develop strong contacts from your group. Or, more immediately, your goal may be just to learn more about the individuals within the group to determine whether it is a valuable source of long-term contacts. Maybe you just want to expand the number of contacts in a particular group. Jot down the networking goals you hope to achieve. For example:

Neighborhood association: Offer to host a neighborhood watch meeting. Join the welcoming committee.

Camp committee: Sign up to host the orientation day festivities.

Conclusion

The process of identifying and evaluating your core network may be tedious, or it may even feel contrived. After all, you've probably always thought of your relationships with people as *relationships*, and your affiliations with organizations have usually been motivated by a personal interest.

But quality relationships and shared interests don't cease to exist when you adopt a networking lifestyle. If anything, they will be enhanced—because if you're truly networking, you'll be looking for ways to *give* something to your contacts and strengthen your relationships. The process of identifying and evaluating your contacts opens many new possibilities because it lays the foundation for growing and expanding your network, which is our next step.

Personal contacts

Name_____Phone_____
Connection_____
Contact's contacts_____

Networking history_____
_____
_____
_____
_____

Quality of contact_____

Goals for contact_____
_____
_____
_____
_____

Name_____Phone_____
Connection_____
Contact's contacts_____

Networking history_____
_____
_____
_____

Quality of contact_____

Goals for contact_____
_____
_____
_____
_____

Community and professional contacts

Name of group_____

Number of/type of individuals involved_____

_____

_____

Networking potential_____

_____

_____

_____

Networking goals_____

_____

_____

_____

Opportunities for further involvement (committees, events, etc.)_____

_____

_____

_____

_____

Name of group_____

Number of/type of individuals involved_____

_____

_____

Networking potential_____

_____

_____

_____

Networking goals_____

_____

_____

_____

Opportunities for further involvement (committees, events, etc.)_____

_____

_____

_____

_____

Personal contacts

List individuals you consider to be your most important networking connections, as well as those you'd like to develop further.

Name *Nora Dorman*

Connection *Editor in Chief, Vacation Horizons magazine*

Contact's contacts *Went to Metropolitan from 4-year position with University Press, knows current editor. University Press uses freelance editors.*

Networking history *1.) I gave her a lead and a recommendation on job opening on staff, where she is now the editor. 2.) She's given me several story assignments for the magazine.*

Quality of contact *Strong contact for work, information, advice, support.*

Goals for contact *Maintain relationship, continue to do freelance articles for magazine.*

Name *Irv. Kane*

Connection *Executive Director, Community Center*

Contact's contacts *Broad base of community contacts. Excellent resource.*

Networking history *1.) I've used him as a reference. 2.) He has asked if I need part-time work. 3.) I've done volunteer committee work for Community Center.*

Quality of contact *Light. Needs development.*

Goals for contact *Develop as referral source for freelance business and future job search.*

Community and professional contacts

Name of group Advertising Club

Number of/type of individuals involved 400 members throughout the city, primarily designers and salespeople.

Networking potential Great group for matchmaking leads and referrals, because most members are designers — team with designers on contract basis.

Networking goals Meet designers and develop freelance team relationships.

Opportunities for further involvement (committees, events, etc.) Join promotions committee and team with designers on development of direct mail precis promoting club functions.

Name of group Fairview Neighborhood Association

Number of/type of individuals involved Association serves as forum for neighborhood affairs in Fairview area, population 6,500.

Networking potential Membership available due to location of my home. Leadership of organization largely drawn from upper-middle class neighborhood that is home to many executives of area corporations. Potentially a good matchmaking and referral source, although considerable effort would have to be invested as no contacts exist now.

Networking goals Attend future meetings and assess networking potential.

Opportunities for further involvement (committees, events, etc.) Consider newsletter committee involvement.

Chapter 7

Expanding
your network

Now that you've identified and evaluated your network, you should be feeling more confident of your networking savvy. Hopefully you've discovered that you have a strong base of core contacts with whom you interact regularly—such as a few co-workers, the members of your volunteer group and/or a neighbor who shares your passion for gardening. You're pleased to have learned that you've actually built up some networking history—perhaps in the form of a job referral, a couple of client recommendations or some valued negotiation tips from a seasoned co-worker.

But through the evaluation process, you probably identified some weak spots as well—some areas that could be developed further. For example, you may have included the name of a networking contact you consider to be well-connected; you have infrequent contact with this person, and you'd like to develop the relationship further. Or perhaps you belong to a professional group that you really haven't tapped into. You attend the monthly luncheons, but you rarely meet new people, and you're frankly wondering if the annual dues are worth it.

You're ready to strengthen your network—to begin *developing and expanding it.*

Whom do your contacts know?
Tapping into your network's networks

It's basic, it's low-tech and it's extremely effective—word-of-mouth advertising. It's also one of the best methods for finding a job; according to the experts, up to 80 percent of all jobs are landed through word-of-mouth referrals. And fortunately, it's at the core of networking. Whether you're looking for an employer, clients, employees, information sources or supporters, you can tap into your existing network, use or generate word-of-mouth advertising, and you'll likely find a seemingly endless web of connections.

No matter what you're looking for, you'll probably want to begin by asking your matchmaking connections for assistance. The secret to getting what you need is to be specific: Target your request.

A direct approach is usually best: "I'm seeking a job the field of environmental law...(or) information about computer training...(or) a sponsor for membership in the Economics Club. I thought that with your contacts you may know someone who might be able to help me achieve this goal." *Don't* approach a matchmaker with some vague request to introduce you to others, or just say "I'm looking for a job." Help your contacts help you by being as specific as possible about what you are seeking.

When I attended a local chapter meeting for Business Network Intl., I was impressed with the way president David Lovell opened the meeting, asking members as they introduced themselves to identify what specific leads they were looking for that particular week. When it came to David's turn, he introduced his business (he sells promotional items—everything from sun visors with corporate logos to coffee mugs to beach towels). I probably know a handful of individuals who have decision-making ability to buy David's products, but not until he identified his current lead goal—talking to people who run summer camp programs to see if he could supply them with caps, towels, T-shirts, etc.—did I see a match. I immediately thought of my son's summer camp.

—B

Although the direct approach is fine, don't use a high-pressure approach such as: "Do you know anyone who can give me a job?" It's a bit like asking a neighbor if she can fix you up with a husband.

If your matchmaker is willing to put you in touch with one of her contacts, she may make the introduction directly—at a meeting, event or arranged meeting—or she may just offer to pave the way for the contact, calling the contact to notify her that you want to meet. According to networking author Melissa Giovagnoli, the value of your matchmaker's referral is the trust she has established with the contact you want to meet. "Through their word and the use of their name," Giovagnoli says, "there is a transference of trust" from the matchmaker to you.

So, now you need to follow up with a phone call in which you introduce yourself, immediately identifying the connection. "Hi. Bev Ginsberg? My name's Molly Ahearn and I'm calling you on the recommendation of my good friend and former co-worker Jim Simon."

Most likely, Bev's reaction will be a friendly "ahh" of recognition, or perhaps a remark like, "Oh yes, Jim told me about you when we had lunch a couple days ago." But you can usually count on an open and listening attitude from this point on in the conversation.

You are now entering one of the most important parts of the conversation—the bridge between the introduction and your request for a meeting. Should you try to establish rapport by engaging in small talk, or assume that your contact is busy and move directly to the business you want to accomplish? There are many ways to handle this, but the focus of your concern should be the contact, from whom you should take your cues, gauging the conversation accordingly. It takes experience and finesse to become an expert at this, but don't worry—as you gain networking experience, you'll become adept at listening to and interpreting your contact's cues.

In the meantime, there is one thing you *should* do: Ask if you have reached your contact at a good time. Phone etiquette dictates that the person who begins the conversation should end it; if your contact is pressed for time, you have given her the opportunity to say so gracefully.

Assuming all indications are "go" for speaking with your contact, you'll ultimately want to direct the conversation toward the reason for your call. Depending upon the nature of the connection—whether it's a potential employer or client, or someone who can provide you with information—you may approach the call differently. In most cases, some sort of a meeting, often referred to as an *informational interview*, is probably appropriate. Try to schedule some time with your contact, preferably at a neutral location such as a restaurant and not at either of your offices. Here are a few examples of how to handle such a request:

> *"Bev, Jim tells me you've had some fascinating experiences working in environmental law. I am interested in specializing in the field, and I was wondering if I could speak to you about the development of your career. May I take you to lunch sometime soon?"*

> *"Bev, Jim told me your institution recently went to a wide-area computer network, and that all your employees received training before your offices went online. I'm researching the possibility of putting in such a system at my office, but I'm concerned about training employees. Would you have an hour to meet with me and discuss your experience, perhaps over coffee?"*

"Bev, Jim tells me you are vice president of membership for the Economics Club. I've always been interested in the organization, especially the lectures the club presents. But I've never had the opportunity to attend a meeting, and I don't know any members who could sponsor me. Would you have a chance to meet with me sometime soon, so that I could learn more about the Club and its programs?"

In selecting a site to meet with your contact, comfort and convenience are important. You want an opportunity to know this person better, which is why an informal location such as a restaurant is better than either of your offices.

Nonetheless, informality doesn't mean it's okay to fly by the seat of your pants—be prepared for your informational interview. Jot down some questions, and do any research that seems necessary. Dress professionally and conduct yourself professionally.

And *listen*. Informational interviews do offer you a chance to tell the contact about yourself, but you're the host. Your attention needs to be focused on your guest.

If you feel you have built good rapport, you may want to ask your contact for advice or indirect assistance. For example, you could ask, "Bev, is there anyone else I should speak to about this topic?" or "Do you have any specific recommendations for me on how I should prepare for a career in this field?" Unless you have had strong indications to the contrary, don't ask for direct assistance at this point, such as "Could you help me find a job?" or even "Would you keep me in mind if you have an opening soon?" It's too soon.

At the end of the meeting, make certain you say thank you, offer your business card and request one from the contact. You will probably also want to ask for permission to keep in touch: "I'm so glad I met you. You can't imagine how helpful you've been to me and I've really enjoyed getting to know you. Would it be okay if I keep in touch with you?"

After the meeting, send one thank-you note to the contact and another to the matchmaker who put you in touch with her. It's a small thing, but it makes a difference. For more on networking etiquette, see Chapter 9.

Getting more out of the groups you belong to: Meet more people at meetings or functions

If you feel that your involvement in groups isn't paying off in terms of networking, maybe the fault lies with you. Are you attending meetings with people you already know? When you walk in with people you already know, or run to grab a seat beside them, you're missing out on an opportunity to make new contacts. Here are a few tips on how to meet more people:

- Shy? Use your acquaintances as leverage. Ask them to introduce you to new people—or introduce them to strangers.
- Offer to be on a welcoming committee. Chances are you'll wear a name badge or be given some official responsibility for greeting members. For some reason, this scary task becomes more palatable under the guise of the group's official business.
- Get there early—it can be less intimidating to approach someone new when the room isn't already crowded with people laughing and talking.

You need to get over whatever it is that's keeping you from broadening your connections. Before attending the next meeting, make a personal goal to introduce yourself to five new people, or to have at least one follow-up contact with a new person. *Make* these meetings work for you. Because if they're don't, they aren't worth the dues.

Wear a name badge

The pre-lunch crowd is buzzing and hovering near tables. You're slightly nervous, and you feel the forced smile start to wear on your jaw muscles. Suddenly, a man pops into your field of vision, jerks out his hand and spouts out his name—or so you assume. You respond by rote with your name and some comment about the great turnout. After a few minutes, you both relax a little—and find out you have some things in common, including a mutual friend. You realize this is a relationship you'd like to consider further, but there's one problem. You have no idea what this guy's name is. If only he were wearing a name tag.

It's certainly not the worst thing in the world to have to ask someone's name again, though it is embarrassing. And isn't it possible that others have been reluctant to ask *your* name when you neglected to wear a name badge? Rather than admit that they'd forgotten it, they simply walked away, smiling and telling you how nice it was to meet you. Perhaps they even remembered you later. "Oh yes, I met a very nice woman the other day at the industry luncheon. I bet she would have been interested in bidding on this job. Too bad I didn't catch her name."

Wear a name tag whenever possible. If it's any type of a business function, include the name of your business as well. People don't remember your name after an introduction about half the time, so have it in front of them all the time. In addition to helping others remember your name, your name tag can be a conversation-starter as well. "Oh, I just met someone else from your company. It must be a large firm." "Hey, you're with Big Deal Enterprises? I just read an article about your company in the paper today. Did you see it?" Or even, "My mother's name was Betsy."

What should you do if you are at a name tag-less networking event? (Horrors!) Well, after you've made a mental note to extol the virtues of name tags to the organizers, you must hunker down and deal with the situation at hand. When people introduce themselves, listen carefully for their names, and then try to use the name in conversation. For example, you could say "Gina, is this the first time you've attended a Networking International event?" Another natural way to help remember the name is to introduce the person to others.

Of course, the exchange of business cards becomes even more important in the absence of name tags, which is why we address it next. We share a number of pointers on the proper way to exchange cards, but as you exchange them, you have a golden opportunity to get a good look at the person's name.

Make business cards work for you

Your business card represents you, so do whatever you can to make sure it does its job well. If you own your own business (or have the creative latitude to order cards that suit you), make sure you consider the copy, design and paper stock carefully. Your card should be clear and easy to read. And, no matter who you work for, carry an ample supply of cards at all times.

One important note for women regarding the information given on your business card: If you are self-employed, you may want to consider using a commercial mail service for your business address, especially if you work from your home. Many women feel it's a wise safety precaution, offering you a measure of protection in the event that you meet someone who has more than a business relationship in mind. In addition, it's probably best to go with a commercial mail service as opposed to a U.S. Post Office box. Deserved or not, where small businesses are concerned, U.S. Post Office boxes carry a stigma that suggests instability—or even a fly-by-night operation. (Commercial mail services typically offer a street address.)

Once you have your cards, make sure you always have an ample supply on hand. If you forget or run out, the results can be embarrassing, as public relations professional Anne Robinson discovered shortly after starting a job with a Midwestern museum. "Within two weeks of starting my new job, I attended one of our region's largest cultural fairs. Over the course of four hours, I met hundreds of people, many of whom worked for other arts or education organizations. A number of people were interested in collaborating on programs and asked for my card. Unfortunately, although my cards had been ordered, they hadn't come in yet. It was an embarrassing situation, and who knows how many valuable contacts I lost?"

The all-important business card exchange

The business card itself is only a tool—exchanging cards with others is more of an art. To do it well, you must first understand that in most situations, business cards do not serve the purpose of introduction in American business culture. While there are certainly exceptions to the norm (for instance, when you're involved in a large meeting with people representing different organizations), business cards are primarily used to signal a continued interest following the introductory conversation.

When you meet someone in the course of business or at a networking event, you should try to find out a little bit about the person and his or her business. Alice Ostrower, who teaches a college course in business communications etiquette, has an approach that's simple but effective—just say to the other person "Tell me a little bit about what you do." Try to find a commonality with the person. The benefit of finding out about the person before you ask for his or her card is that there will be times when you don't want future contact. As soon as you know this, try to move on.

If you do find common ground with the person, look for ways to follow up, and then ask for the person's card. For example, you could say, "I know of a wonderful article on computers and the future of small businesses, perhaps I could send it to you. May I have your card?" More often than not, your request for a card will prompt the new contact to reciprocate by requesting yours.

Get it down on paper

As your networking activity increases, you will need to develop a system for collecting and dispensing cards. Many people choose a two-case system—one for cards you collect from others and one for holding your own cards.

You can use the cards you collect to note information about the contacts. Devise your own system for what to write. Many people prefer to note functional information, such as where they met the contact and the name of the person who introduced them. Others write their ideas for follow-up with the contact. For example, if you learn from a conversation with Betsy Sheldon that she has co-authored a book about networking, make a note: "Networking author—maybe she'll speak to my department!" Still others believe that shorter is better, as long as it works to remind you of whom you got the card from; physical information like "short redhead" may be enough of a reminder.

When it comes to making these notes, you will need to assess the nature of the situation and decide whether it's appropriate. If you've promised to forward someone an article, making a note on the back of her card while you talk should enhance the impression you make by indicating you're likely to follow through. But if you're at an event with a more formal atmosphere, you may decide it's inappropriate to whip out your pen and make notes. If you need to capture the information, but sense that it's not the atmosphere for taking notes, move to a discreet location.

On the other hand, if you're attending a large trade show, the sole purpose of which is to generate business, it's probably appropriate—and smart—to turn over the card and make the note then. After all, you can collect so many cards at events like these that remembering who's who at the end of the day is impossible!

Look for ways to follow up the introduction

Your professional group's meeting is winding down, and you have met two great contacts who could assist you in a job search. You exchanged business cards, so you're set, right? Perhaps. But when it comes to business, there's no substitute for certainty. Wouldn't it be better to leave the meeting knowing that you'll keep in touch?

When you meet a new contact, try not to walk away without committing to some sort of future contact. You don't have to become best buddies in the five minutes that remain, but there are simple ways to give a new business relationship momentum. Here are a few ideas:

- "I've got an article about that topic I think you'd find interesting. I'll send you a copy."
- "I'm anxious to know how that event turns out for you. Mind if I call you afterward to see if you felt it was worthwhile?"

- "I'll let you know if I can think of any other suppliers who have that expertise."
- "That project sounds very intriguing—and similar to something I'm trying to propose at my company. I'd like to follow up with another conversation. Could I call you for lunch sometime?"
- "I hope to see you at the next meeting. Maybe we can even grab a lunch table together."

Get more involved

Another great way to get more networking impact out of the groups you belong to is to do more than just show up to the regular functions. Join a planning committee, plan special events or offer to write articles for the group newsletter. Do whatever it takes to circulate, gain more visibility and make connections with more people.

Some of the most powerful networking contacts you can make are those that come from serving with others, whether it's a professional or community organization. Your new contacts have an opportunity to see you in action, and they come away with a sense of your skills and abilities. You're working together toward a common goal, and building a relationship. Compare the following referrals. If the subject was you, which would you prefer?

"I met a marketing writer—Joyce Hadley. She's in my Freelance Forum group. I've talked to her a couple times at meetings. She seems like she'd be pretty good."

"You should call Joyce Hadley, a writer who contributes regularly to our newsletter. She always meets deadlines. Her writing is really strong and rarely requires editing. I think you'll like her."

There's really only one risk to this contact-building strategy. If you commit to something, carry it through. Don't leave the very people you're trying to impress holding the bag.

Take on more responsibility at work

Just when you feel you can't take on one more responsibility on the job, we suggest you help with projects that *don't* directly pertain to your job?

Do it—it will be worth it. Particularly if you work for a company that has many departments and employees, getting involved in projects outside your department and narrow realm of responsibility will maximize your networking opportunities on the job.

Many corporations and institutions use employee task forces or project groups for input on issues from evaluating a new phone system to developing a corporate drug policy to preparing for the annual Christmas party. Raise your hand and say "Me! Me!" when opportunities like these arise. It's your chance to expand your network within the company. These types of activities allow you to showcase your talents to co-workers who might otherwise be lucky to know your name.

And, if downsizing strikes, you'll be in a better position if you have strong contacts in other areas of the company. Chances are, even if your department is decimated, your contacts on the computer conversion task force will remember your diligence and attention to detail, and they'll try to find you a place in another department. This network-building strategy will increase your visibility and influence within the organization, and offer you a form of unemployment insurance you can't get anywhere.

Join new groups

In order to have a diversity of networking contacts, it's necessary to have diversity in your involvement. If you belong to five industry organizations, but you aren't involved in any community groups or informal networks, chances are you're running into the same people—or at least the same types of people, and you're not maximizing your networking potential.

Your networking mix will be unique; it depends upon your career, your goals, your personality and communication style. There's no prescribed formula (such as one business leads group, two industry associations, two community groups, etc.). Nonetheless, there are a few rules of thumb to consider:

- Don't belong to so many groups that your schedule is packed with meetings. You want time to develop relationships from those groups.

- Evaluate your involvements for both the quantity and quality of networking contacts they provide. Professional groups may offer many potential contacts during a job search, but becoming involved in a community organization has a direct networking benefit for you and another for the company you represent, which in turn benefits your position within your company.

- Limit your affiliation with business leads groups to one to avoid a conflict of interests.

Evaluate a group before joining

Once you've decided which types of groups you're interested in joining, you'll want to explore a few of each kind before you commit yourself. Use your existing network, and ask your contacts for their help. Do they know others who belong to the groups you're considering? As you gather information about various groups, here are some questions to consider:

1. How will this group serve your current needs? (Are you looking for a job? Building a business or client list? Searching for information?) How will it serve your long-term interests?

2. How will it fit with the other organizations you belong to? Is there a potential conflict of interest? Do you already belong to a similar organization?

3. Is the group well-established? Does it have a good reputation?

4. What is the cost—and what do you get for it? (Workbooks, access to benefits, training, etc.) Will the investment pay off?

5. How many members are in the group? In the chapter? Will you be exposed to enough contacts to make it worth your while?

6. Who are the members? Are they the types of people who will share similar beliefs, values, experiences or business ethics?

7. Does the group place emphasis on business integrity?

8. How often does the group meet? What are attendance requirements? Are they realistic for you?

9. What is the structure of the meetings? Loose and informal or structured and rigid?

10. What are the key objectives of the group? Is it primarily social? Philanthropic? Self-serving?

11. What are the member requirements? Can you meet them? Do you need a sponsor?

12. Are there any additional time commitments that you must meet?

13. What is the "feel" of the group? When you attended a meeting as a guest, did you feel welcomed—or ignored?

14. What do its members say about their experiences? (Try to talk to a few away from the meeting.)

In order to find the answers to these questions, take the following actions:

1. Get brochures, magazines, newsletters and any printed materials you can find about the group you are considering joining.
2. Attend a meeting or function, preferably two or more. (Some limit the number of functions you can attend without joining.)
3. Talk to several members—even former members. Find out the good and bad.
4. Check out the group's competition as well.

Get off to a good start

The first few times you attend a group meeting, do your best to arrive early. Introduce yourself to the president and officers, and ask to be introduced to other members. Use your listening skills. Focus on those you are speaking with and be gracious. Try to make the person you are speaking with feel comfortable, and you're less likely to feel self-conscious. Smile, make eye contact and offer a firm handshake whenever you are introduced to someone. And don't forget to bring an ample supply of your business cards.

Getting involved in the group will help you feel more at home, so try to do it as soon as you can. (Of course, you thought about volunteering for the organization before you joined, knowing it was the best way to get involved and meet people, so you're quite sure you have the time.) It's not necessary to head a committee right from the start, as you'll need to learn the group's culture. Give yourself time to learn how you fit in, and have fun in the process.

Create a board of advisers

You don't have to own a business to benefit from a board of advisers. And it doesn't have to be as formal as it sounds. In fact, the members of your board don't even have to know they're serving. The important thing is that you formalize the concept of your core network in your mind, and come to see the members of your network in an advisory capacity.

Take a look at your core network and ask yourself if it fulfills your needs. What types of support, input, information and feedback do you need? You may already have a mentor or two. Perhaps you need some matchmakers, a supporter or the advice of an expert in a particular field, such as accounting or office technologies. If you need a different point of view, is there someone who will really tell it like it is, even if it's not something you want to hear?

Chances are, you can identify a position on your ideal board that needs to be filled. Perhaps you have discovered that most of the people in your core network come from the same circle. You may need to reach out to new people and "appoint" some new advisers.

It's not necessary to have board meetings. Simply identifying these people and keeping in regular contact with them will get you in the right mindset. But meeting with individuals on a regular basis is important. It's also important to thank your advisers for their help and reciprocate in any way you can.

Create your own networking group

Suppose you're doing everything right, but the support, information and/or contacts you need are just not available through existing networking groups. Why not start your own group, dedicated to providing whatever it is that you can't otherwise find?

That's exactly what Kim Hackett of Indianapolis did in 1991, following the birth of her first child. The Women's Home Business Network (WHBN) began as an informal association of women who work at home. They held their first meetings at a branch of the local library, hoping to meet other women in similar situations, exchange ideas, offer support and advice and make connections.

Today, WHBN is an incorporated nonprofit organization with 175 members and five chapters in the Indianapolis area, and it plans to expand nationwide. The group promotes and supports home-based businesses by offering educational programs on topics from marketing to taxes, retirement investing to small claims court. In addition to the monthly meeting topic, each gathering features 10-minute "spotlights" for individual members' businesses.

Speaking of the phenomenal success of the idea, Hackett says, "We've inadvertently tapped into an overwhelming need. As a women's organization, we're filling a particular niche that others aren't. A lot of women are frustrated by balancing home responsibilities with rigid corporate structure, so they're leaving to start their own businesses." She says members come to meetings "to learn things, meet other entrepreneurs and to share frustrations and successes. The result is...we do a lot of business with each other."

But the Women's Home Business Network also fills another important need that other networking organizations don't. WHBN allows its members to be themselves and do business networking on their own terms. Hackett notes that many women are intimidated by the corporate feel of other groups, with "women dressed in suits and doing an aggressive networking thing. They don't like having to turn into men in order to do business. A lot of women are going into business (for themselves) to get *away* from that."

The success of the WHBN concept notwithstanding, perhaps the networking group you have in mind is less formal in concept. If the goal is nurturing your network, then meeting contacts once a month for dinner and conversation can be just as effective.

"Solitary confinement" might best describe my first two months as a home-based writer and editor. Although I loved the flexibility my new situation afforded, I missed the creative stimulation, the exchange of ideas and humor—even popping into the cubicles of my co-workers to share news from the office grapevine. I even started looking forward to visits from my UPS courier.

As an antidote to this social deprivation, I initiated a gathering of several former co-workers, all who'd started their own endeavors. We met at the end of the workday at a favorite restaurant, shared stories, caught up on personal happenings, passed along leads and exchanged experiences. Despite its unstructured format, the first meeting was an overwhelming networking success! Three attendees walked away with new business, one woman gained some valuable information on an industry organization she was considering joining and another learned of an upcoming workshop she'd otherwise have missed. We continue to meet not-quite-monthly, and all seem to prefer the loose structure.

Why has this informal group been so successful for us? For one thing, we really like each other. We also share a work history; when we refer one another, we can offer legitimate testimony as to the quality of each other's work. And finally, we share a commonality—we're all struggling and reveling in the trials and joys of self-employment.

—B

If the idea of starting your own group appeals to you, consider carefully the following issues before you grab the phone and start calling people:

1. What are your current needs? (Industry information? Leads? Support?) And how do you see this group fulfilling those needs?
2. What are your long-term needs, and how do you see this group fulfilling those?

3. How will this group be different from other groups you currently belong to?
4. Identify in a sentence or two, or in a few key points, the primary objectives of this group.
5. What is an ideal number of people for this group?
6. Whom do you know that would "fit" with the group and its goals?
7. What types of people would you recruit for your group? Mentors, matchmakers or supporters? Seasoned professionals? Individuals representing different fields? Men? Women?
8. How often should the group meet? Weekly? Monthly?
9. What is the structure of the meeting? Loose and informal or structured and rigid?

Obviously, if you determine that a more structured format is desired, you'll need to do a lot more work, perhaps even considering having officers, taking minutes, establishing member requirements, requiring dues, creating printed materials, planning agendas and more.

Rather than doing all this startup work yourself, you might want to draw on the support of a national network, such as the National Association for Female Executives (NAFE). As a member, you can establish a local network under the NAFE umbrella—but as a separate entity. The organization provides you with support and guidance. You're free to establish and run the group as you and the members see fit. NAFE does have a few requirements of its affiliated networks. Among them: You must make a commitment to lead a group of at least 20 members, individuals who are also national NAFE members, and you must submit semiannual reports.

For more information on NAFE networks, refer to the NAFE address and phone number in the resources section at the end of this book.

Conclusion

There are limitless ways to expand your network, from tried-and-true approaches like joining and participating in professional organizations, to simply meeting for a pleasant evening with colleagues. But expanding your network does require effort. You must develop a mindset and *make* things happen— you have to *think* "connect" all the time. Know your goals, be open and reach out, and you'll find that your network will grow.

Chapter 8

Maintaining
your network

At some point during your childhood, whether you learned it from your parents or a teacher, you no doubt came to understand that privileges are almost always accompanied by responsibilities. The maxim is certainly true of networking: If you have the privilege of claiming a networking relationship with someone, you also have a responsibility to work at maintaining the relationship. Put simply, if you only call your contacts when you need them, it won't be long before they no longer need you. But how do you approach maintaining something as abstract as a network of human relationships?

Keep track of your networking

As with any task, if you want to succeed at networking, you have to analyze and organize your activity. A certain percentage of readers will do this with ease, while the rest of us may prefer to run for cover. If you're thinking of lacing up your shoes, don't. Even experts like Susan Hailey, director of business development and planning for Resumix, a Silicon Valley software company, find this difficult. "I keep my network fairly alive, but not nearly as alive as when I'm doing a job search. I have to be honest about that," she says, adding, "But I've been trying to keep it going anyway, especially now that I'm at a place where I'm fairly stable and happy doing what I'm doing."

All you really need to keep your network alive is a sincere desire to make it work and the discipline to structure it. Don't worry though, you needn't develop the skills of an air traffic controller to manage your networking activity. But you do need a system, and your system begins with two basic tools:

1. **A list of your contacts.** Choose the system that suits you, but make sure you pull the information together. Common tools for listing your contacts and their phone numbers include a telephone-address book, Rolodex, business card box or computer program.

2. A calendar. You *must* keep track of meetings, appointments, programs and luncheons. Use a calendar, a Day-Timer, a running to-do list or a computer-generated list. And don't limit your notations to engagements. You need to schedule follow-up activity as well.

In addition, you might consider a computer software system, such as ACT for Windows, to assist you with tracking your activity. Recommended by several networking pros, it's a contact management program that lists the members of your network along with vital information about them. It tracks your networking activity (with your assistance, of course)—and even reminds you of when you should follow up with specific contacts. (There are other contact management programs, but ACT is the one that most of the people we interviewed recommended. For more information, see the resources section.)

One great benefit of such programs is that many allow you to input key words to search your networking database. For example, if you're unable to remember the name of the person you met from the Mayor's Arts Council, you could input the word "Arts" and get a list of names that contain that word as part of their description.

If you don't use a program like ACT, you'll need to develop your own system for keeping track of activity. Perhaps you could adapt the worksheets we included in Chapter 6 for personal, community and professional contacts.

Follow-up activity

Most of us couldn't survive in the real world without scheduling our meetings and appointments. We look at monthly, weekly and daily schedules. We set appointments on the minute, even computing drive time.

Yet many of us neglect to schedule inquiries or courtesies, although these are equally important. Have you ever forgotten to do something about a friend or co-worker's birthday because you noted the day on your calendar, but made no advance notation to buy a card or arrange to meet her for lunch?

And what about that article you promised to send to the president of the local chapter of Women in Communications? Perhaps you wrote it on your to-do list and sent it. But did you call her a week or so later to see if she received it? If not, you may have missed a valuable opportunity to follow up with a new contact. That's exactly the type of problem that scheduling your follow-up activity will eliminate. And it's an easy, commonsense concept. There are just a few pointers to share:

1. If you have met someone for the first time, write your action commitment on the back of their business card at your first opportunity. Then transfer the information to your Day-Timer or calendar as soon as you can.

2. If you commit to doing something for someone, be sure to do it. Get into the habit of carrying a Day-Timer or to-do list everywhere so you can make immediate notes of commitments you take on, whether calling for an appointment, sending a fax or contacting a new lead following a network referral.

3. You're not done just because you did what you promised to do. Make a note to call and check the results of your action. Did your new contact have a chance to call the advertising agency you recommended? Did your referral result in a job interview?

Helping others helps you

Following up is not merely a process of creating and executing an action checklist. Keeping the exchange alive is an important part of the networking concept. Therefore, follow-up also includes finding new ways to assist long-time members of your network. Could you help your counterpart in ad sales if you mentored one of her new employees? Perhaps one of your mentors is a telecommunications professor at a local college. Could you volunteer to help with their annual fund raising campaign?

Take a look at the people who make up your core network, and list things you could do to help each of them. Then make it happen, and watch as your network gains strength. The more you invest in your network, the more your network will reward you.

Maintain your extended network

All of us have contacts with whom we no longer have formal ties. They are the former co-workers who moved on to other jobs, the vendors and clients who moved into new businesses and the friends who have simply moved. Think of these contacts as your "extended network."

It takes effort to maintain any relationship, and networking relationships are no exception. If you want your connection to survive, you'll have to do more than send a Christmas card—you'll need to take action.

Keeping in touch with your extended network can be great fun. If you still live close to one another, perhaps you could meet every month for dinner. Keep your eye out for natural ways to make contact, then pick up the phone. For example:

- You read something about your contact's recent promotion in the local business paper and called to congratulate him.
- You ran into a mutual acquaintance and it made you realize you hadn't talked in a while, so you called to see how things were going.
- You saw an article or heard some information that you knew would be of interest to him.
- There's an event you think he might attend, and you called to see if you can expect him there. Perhaps you could meet.

If this approach doesn't prompt you to get in touch within a reasonable time (two months or so), then you need to be proactive. Make a note on your calendar or plug the time window into your software program, but make sure you call to see how things are going. If the call only amounts to a friendly chat that's okay, but if an opportunity for follow-up action presents itself, then go for it. Things to look for include:

- Opportunities to get together.
- A chance to send some information.
- A chance to answer a question your contact might have.

But what about your long-distance contacts? Distance needn't be an impediment to a good networking relationship. As a matter of fact, the authors of this book are networking contacts who stay in touch (even when we're *not* scrambling on a book deadline) via phone, fax and Federal Express. Although we haven't lived in the same state for more than 10 years, we've remained closely connected and have shared work, advice and leads during this time.

And of course, there's a technological revolution underway that's adding a global dimension to networking. It's the Internet—a global network that links more than 25,000 computer networks, including everything from mainframe systems to personal computers. Using the Internet for networking deserves a book of its own, but there's one aspect everyone needs to keep their eye on— e-mail.

If you have a computer with a modem and an Internet connection available (via a local dial-up service or commercial service) then you have the opportunity to communicate with any one of 20 million people around the world. And, in most cases, once you pay the monthly charge to your service, sending and receiving of messages is free. How much easier could it be to stay in touch with your friend on sabbatical in New Zealand?

Chances are, if you have e-mail, you're probably already using it to keep in touch with others who are online. If you don't have e-mail, it's certainly something to keep in mind. It can link you to local and international contacts with equal ease.

But no matter what, distance is no reason for losing touch with a valuable contact. E-mail offers convenient and immediate transfer of your message, but a handwritten note sent via "snail-mail" (Internet-speak for the post office) is just as effective.

How often should you try to make contact?

"Okay, okay," you say..."I'll keep in touch. But how often is often enough?" The answer to that question depends upon many things. It depends on how active the relationship is, how long you've known the person, the strength of the relationship and the type of contact you normally have with the person. Is it best to speak briefly on the phone, or is this person someone you should meet for 18 holes of golf?

It's important to do what feels natural in the relationship. With some contacts, such as co-workers, it's appropriate to be in touch daily or weekly. There may be other contacts you only need to see or speak with twice a year.

Making judgments about how often to touch base with your network requires you to cultivate sensitivity to the needs of others. If you're a good listener, you'll develop a sense of what each contact values. Some will want to keep their conversations brief and to the point, while others need to feel a sense of camaraderie and value a supportive relationship. There are no rules; you just need to do what "fits." Just be sure you don't let it go longer than feels right.

Ending networking relationships

Having placed so much emphasis on the maintenance your network, it may seem abrupt to begin a discussion of how and when to end a networking relationship. But no one can maintain an unlimited number of networking relationships. Our careers and lives change, and our relationships must change with them.

Most of the time, proactive endings are not necessary. More often than not, networking relationships end through attrition: You change employers, your contact changes fields or perhaps one of you moves to a new city. Whatever the reason for the change, the end result is that you drift apart.

To get a sense of this, check out your Rolodex from time to time. If you run across the names or business cards of people you can't even remember, it's safe bet that they're not important participants in your network, and it's okay to discard their names.

You will also likely run across names of individuals who may have been important contacts at one time. If you haven't spoken with them for a year or two, ask yourself whether the relationship is worth reactivating. If the answer if yes, or even if you're not sure, call or write a note. If the response is positive and you sense there's some value to staying in touch, keep the name in your file and make an effort to keep in contact, even if it's only every few months or so. And don't forget to *give* something, even if it's something as simple as sending an article or cartoon that reminded you of him or her. It takes more than one action to rekindle a dying fire.

Of course, there are times when ending an interaction requires some effort. Perhaps you have a contact who is abusing the networking relationship, pestering you with requests for advice and referrals and offering nothing in return. You certainly are not obligated to advise or offer referrals to someone you're uneasy with. When this is the case, it's best to be direct but tactful. Simply say, "I'm sorry, but I am not comfortable making that recommendation for you," or "I think you would be better served by asking someone else for advice."

Ending the relationship altogether will require either more firmness or more energy—or both. Many people, especially women, find it difficult to say something blunt like "I really don't want you to contact me in the future," although it's an approach that would almost certainly work. Instead, be gently discouraging each time the person calls, turning down each specific request: "I'm sorry, you've reached me at a busy time, and I simply can't help you now." Don't say anything to encourage future calls, and don't make use of the connection in any way—don't call, don't write and don't ask for assistance.

Ending relationships with organizations

As we grow and change in our careers and personal lives, our associations change, and there may come a time when membership in some groups is no longer productive. For instance, there's probably no need to maintain your Advertising Club membership if you quit your career as a copywriter and are now an attorney. The same holds true if you consistently fail to use the organization for networking opportunities, even though you remain in the field. In both cases, the solution is probably as simple as not rejoining.

There are times, however, when your history with an organization means you have something at stake, even though you don't wish to maintain your membership. Perhaps you are a past board member or once served as the organization's president. Maybe you were recognized as a leader in your field and received the organization's highest award.

Situations like these call for a great deal of tact on your part. Although you may not wish to remain with the group, there's no sense burning your bridges by leaving without explanation. Write a letter to the president, vice president of membership or whomever you feel is appropriate. Thank the organization for giving you the opportunity to serve and tactfully explain that your present commitments do not permit you to be an active participant. Say a gracious good-bye, and go on your way.

Conclusion

Good networking means staying on top of your responsibilities to your contacts. It means looking for ways to keep in touch and helping them in any way you can. Some of your contacts may be people you associate with on a strictly professional level, while others may become mentors, confidants or just plain friends. Maintaining your contact relationships needn't be a formal routine, like scheduling car maintenance. It should be enjoyable. If it's not, then ask yourself whether the contact is one you want to maintain. You should strive for a natural exchange with the members of your network. Learn to recognize when it's happening, when you need to make it happen and when you need to let it go.

Chapter 9

Networking etiquette

Etiquette is a funny topic. Many people avoid the subject because they find it staid and boring. Others feel etiquette is nothing more than a set of antiquated rules, and that in modern society it is more important to act "naturally." Of course, Judith Martin, better known as Miss Manners, passionately believes that acting naturally is one of the worst things we can do, socially speaking. And we couldn't agree more.

True, we have, throughout this book, encouraged you to look for "natural" opportunities to make contact with people, and we have advised you to strive for a "natural" rapport with your members of network. But suggesting that you have a genuine basis for your interactions is not the same as suggesting that you "do what comes naturally." All too often, what comes naturally to us is not the least bit nice. For instance, we would not recommend that you place an annoying caller on hold while you file your nails, although if you're truly frustrated, that might come naturally (and come to think of it, it might work).

Etiquette isn't something you learn so that you will be comfortable socially. It is something you learn so others will be comfortable with you. Etiquette, and its attendant issues of respect, dignity and ethics, are underlying ideas throughout our book. Therefore, it may seem redundant to have a separate chapter on the topic. But because if its importance, we offer it nonetheless, as a refresher, a summary, a reference and, on the off-chance that you thought it was optional, so you'll know that it's not.

Etiquette at networking events

Greeting and meeting new contacts

Overall, it's a good idea to approach all new situations as your opportunity to help someone else. You may recall Andra Brack of Business Network Intl. and her "Can I Possibly Help You?" approach. (Don't fret, if you've forgotten, we're about to remind you.) Brack suggests that in order to get anything from networking you have to be prepared to give something. The "Can I Possibly Help You?" approach is strategically good from the standpoint of networking, and if you're shy, it may offer a way to overcome your inhibitions. As it relates to etiquette, it puts you in the right mindset, as your concern is helping others and making them feel comfortable. This approach is also likely to help you achieve your first goal—establishing rapport.

As for the mechanics of introductions, you need to do all those things your parents taught you:

1. Make eye contact.
2. Smile.
3. Offer a firm handshake.
4. Acknowledge the person by name: "Nice to meet you, Mary."
5. Be sensitive to body language. If you're attending a large affair and the person you're speaking with seems distracted and harried, indicating a desire to move on, allow him or her to do so. "I won't keep you, but I'm hoping we'll have a chance to talk in the future. Your job sounds fascinating and I'd like to hear more about it."
6. Special situations may require you to stand to say hello or for an introduction. This traditional way of showing respect applies when you are introduced to (or greet) someone of significantly higher rank (such as the CEO) or significantly greater age, and it applies to women as well as men. (If you stand to acknowledge another woman because of her age, be *sure* the difference is significant. If she's not that much older than you, your attempt to be polite is more likely to offend her.)

Business cards

The first and perhaps most important rule about business cards is that they are rarely used for the purpose of introduction (one notable exception would be in business meetings). In American business, it is simply considered impolite to shove your business card at the person as you're shaking hands.

According to Susan RoAne, author of *How to Work a Room*, "The exchange of cards should follow a conversation in which rapport has been established." If, in the course of your conversation, you establish a mutual interest that you want to pursue, and the person has requested something from you (such as information or a contact name), then it's appropriate to get your business card and write the requested information on the back.

Suppose you haven't hit upon a reason to offer your card and the person hasn't offered his or hers; yet you're interested in future contact. You might say something like, "In case I think of anything else that might be of interest to you, why don't I get your business card so I can follow up?"

When it comes to exchanging business cards in social situations, it may be wise to exercise a little caution. The lines between business and social entertaining have blurred considerably, and much of the time it's quite all right to mix business with pleasure. Nonetheless, there are individuals who resent being approached on business when they are socializing, and there are occasions when it may not be appropriate to ask for a card.

Regarding people, the best advice we can offer is to trust your intuition and your sense of how the conversation is going. If you've established rapport and are convinced there's a mutual interest in making additional contact, then by all means ask for the card. If the person seems put off by inquiries about his or her work, then you may need to forego the opportunity today. (Perhaps you can come away with enough information to follow up with the person by phone.)

As for the occasion, again, it's often a matter of intuition. One way to deal with the situation is to acknowledge the occasion in your request for a card: "I know this isn't the best time to get into business, but I would like to talk with you further. May I have your card?"

As a final note, according to Emily Post, in many European countries it is customary to exchange cards as part of *all* business introductions. If you do business with people from other countries, you'll need to bear this in mind. If you're traveling on business, you may need to adapt to this custom. One obvious benefit of this convention is that neither party has to ask for the other's card. One drawback, as we'll discuss next, is that someone you don't wish further contact with will know how to reach you.

When you *don't* want to make a connection

Maybe it's your woman's intuition, or maybe it's something less subtle—your new acquaintance and lunch partner just slipped two dinner rolls and a place setting into her bag. Whatever the cause, you've picked up strong warning signs and you're not interested in pursuing any further contact with this individual...yet here *she* is, eagerly asking you for your business card and making efforts to pin you down for a lunch date soon. How do you respond with tact and grace without giving out your card and committing yourself to further involvement with her?

Don't feel obliged to give out your business card if you feel uncomfortable doing so. Business communications etiquette teacher Alice Ostrower says, "I personally stay away from 'hunters.' When they ask me for their business cards, I say 'I just ran out.' "

PR and marketing professional Laura Gates advises a similar approach: "Sometimes I'll say 'I'm getting new cards printed, but if you give me one of your cards, I'd be happy to send you information on my company.' If I feel comfortable with that person, then I'll go ahead and send the information."

A request for a card puts the requestee on the spot, and these strategies offer you a graceful way out. Of course, the risk you run is that the person will see you dispensing your cards to others, so you will need to be very careful during the rest of the networking engagement. And, there's always the possibility that no matter what excuse you offer about your card, the person will offer to just jot your number down.

If she succeeds in cornering you and getting your number, you'll have to deal with the follow-up phase and be politely discouraging when she calls. If you're extremely uncomfortable, you may need to be blunt, saying something like "I'm sorry, I prefer not give out that information." This should not only put an end to the request for a card; it will likely end the conversation as well. A variation on this—one that probably works best with salespeople and suppliers—might be, "This is a very busy time for me, so I would prefer that you didn't call. But could I get your card in case I want to call you back?"

If the contact is pursuing a follow-up meeting with you, politely say, "Gee, this is a bad time for me. I'm afraid I just can't schedule anything right now." Say no more. If she persists and asks *when* you'll be free, be vague and suggest that *she* give you a call in a couple of months. Chances are, she'll have forgotten all about it by then.

How to move on

Miss Manners recently addressed the concerns of a gentle reader distressed over how to break off long-winded conversations at business-related meetings and luncheons. Ever straightforward and no-nonsense, Miss Manners pointed out that as such gatherings are designed for the purpose of meeting many people in a short time, it is entirely appropriate to keep one or two conversations from taking over. She advises, however, that a *polite* networker will offer a strong conclusion to a conversation—rather than a weak excuse.

Good advice, Miss Manners! Indeed, such events are meant for you to meet many others. After all, if your intent was to sneak off to a corner to have an intimate *tête-à-tête* with Marge from Monopolize International, you could have easily scheduled a lunch date for just the two of you.

However, as Miss Manners properly pointed out, there is a "gentle" way to break off a conversation. Her suggestion, "I'm so glad I had a chance to meet you—this was fascinating, and I hope to see you again," is entirely acceptable. You might even be more straightforward: "I'd really like to talk to you longer, but there are some other people I must touch base with. Could we talk on the phone or schedule lunch?" The thing you want to avoid is making excuses, "Oh, I promised my boss I'd be back at the office by one o'clock," or "Oh dear, I just remembered I left my car lights on. Have to run." These are white lies you are easily caught in when you're spotted just a few minutes later chatting idly with another attendee.

Sharing leads

Asking for leads

In the course of a conversation with a relatively new contact, you learn that this person knows the director of marketing for a concert promotion agency. You know the agency will soon undertake development of a new outdoor music venue, and they'll be adding to their marketing staff. This is one referral you would love to have someone make on your behalf.

Although you have only known this person for about two months, you worked together on a special project for a community organization; she's seen you in action and knows a little about your abilities. Should you ask for an introduction?

In this case, go for it. But the scenario illustrates the first of several points of etiquette you should observe when asking members of your network for help:

1. Be sure you have a relationship in which you can ask for this favor. Do you know the person well enough or, rather, does the person know *you* well enough to give you the name?

2. Be specific about your request. In this case, let your contact know you would like to meet the marketing director for Cool Concerts Incorporated so that you can find out more about the company and the promotions they do. You would also like the director to be aware of your interest in the company.

3. Be sensitive to your contact's situation. She may not be in a good position to make the introduction you're seeking, or she may think the timing is poor.

4. If your contact agrees to give you the lead, be sure to follow up. Your contact will have called the individual to prepare him or her for your call. Don't make her look foolish.

5. Thank your contact! The minimum courtesy you should offer is a thank-you note. Your loyal support is also required now and in the future.

Giving out leads

Now the shoe is on the other foot. A person approaches you and asks you to put him or her in touch with someone he or she hopes to a) get a job from, b) sell something to or c) get information or some other favor from. Of course, you want to help, particularly if he or she is a good friend or acquaintance. But the other party you have to be sensitive to is the person who's name he or she is after.

Years ago, I got a phone call from my friend Jim. After exchanging brief greetings, he asked in a hurt tone. "Have I done something to offend you?" "Why, of course not!" I replied, truly baffled. "Then why did you sic your granola friend on me?" he countered. I paused, then burst into laughter. I had indeed given his name to another acquaintance-turned-health-beverage salesman who had pestered me to the point I was avoiding the phone. I was only successful in shaking him off after I gave him the names of Jim and two other acquaintances. Thankfully, Jim and I were on good enough terms that he was willing to accept my apology—and a free dinner. Now that I think about it, I never did hear from the other two acquaintances again.

—B

Avoid giving out the names of people whom you *know* would not appreciate it. If you suspect that the individual requesting the lead is not competent at his or her job, or conducts himself or herself unethically, it will only distress your contact. You can politely refuse the request, saying something like: "I would like to assist you, but I'm uncomfortable doing what you ask at this time," or, "From my understanding of circumstances, that would not be appropriate at this time. If things change, I'll let you know." A sensitive person won't press. And if the person isn't sensitive? Well, then you'll know you've done your friend a big favor.

You can also say something like, "I'm not sure the timing is good for that connection right now. Why don't you let me get a feel for what's going on and I'll get back to you in a couple of days?" If you believe the situation has some potential benefit to your other connection, you can approach him or her. If there's a problem, you'll help both people avoid an unpleasant situation.

If you feel that giving the lead is appropriate, by all means give the requester the name and number. But suggest that he or she give you time to call the contact first, to "red flag" the call. Without this entree, there's a chance that a hurried contact might brush off the caller in an attempt to save time.

If you don't hear back from the requester soon (within a week or so from meeting point), call your contact yourself to make sure things went well. Hopefully, they did, but you don't want to be the last to know if your requester came off as a nudge, a bore, a pest or a no-show.

If things work out well and a new relationship is born, a thank-you note to your contact wouldn't be out of line. "I'm glad things worked out to your mutual benefit. I know Tony is a terrific designer and I'm sure you'll be happy with his work. And thanks for making me a hero! Tony's so appreciative of the introduction to you, I think he'll be taking me to lunch for the next month!"

Writing notes

Acknowledgments

When you acknowledge the activities of your networking contacts—whether a promotion, an award or merely some media recognition—you do a lot to solidify the mortar that binds your relationship. Small efforts like a phone call or a quick note speak volumes, conveying the Hallmark sentiment, "I'm thinking of you."

In the early days of my upstart career as a magazine editor and writer, I worked for a company of 1,500 people, many of whom I had rare interaction with, as the publishing arm of the business was sort of sequestered from the rest of the activity. Yet, each time I received a promotion, or earned an industry award, I'd receive a brief, handwritten note from one particular executive vice president. That a man who had the ear of the CEO on a daily basis took the time to acknowledge my humble successes made a strong impression on me, and I became a loyal supporter.

—B

Send a note or call when you read something about a contact in the newspaper. For example, you read in the business column that an associate just received a promotion. Cut it out and attach a note. What other types of things should you acknowledge?

- Promotions.
- Awards.
- Media coverage in which your contact is interviewed.
- Media coverage about the business, industry or even personal interests of your contact.
- Any instance in which you learn you have a mutual acquaintance.

If you hate to write notes, but love to talk on the phone, you may be tempted to call exclusively. But be warned, notes are usually more effective. For one thing, they're less intrusive, and your message can't be diluted by getting off onto conversational tangents. (Example: "Hey, that was a great interview in the *Business Weekly*! Oh, and will you be at the association lunch next week?) A note is also a keepsake. There are many who like to keep such things, perhaps even hanging them on a bulletin board. And a note says more about the effort you put into the relationship.

Note-writing is a great habit to get into, and one you'll want to cultivate— although it may be difficult to implement at first. Here are some pointers:

1. Start by stocking up on note cards, including both thank-you and generic types. If you always have a supply on hand, you're more likely to seize the moment and write a note. If, on the other hand, you tell yourself you'll send a note as soon as you pick up some cards, chances are you'll never do it.

2. Keep a supply of cards in your briefcase or purse. If you're stuck waiting for the doctor or on an airplane, you can utilize the time.

3. Schedule your note-writing on a weekly basis. There may be times you don't have any notes to write, but it's better to schedule the time than to have it squeezed out.

4. Keep your addresses and a supply of stamps handy—in your briefcase with your note supply. You may want to keep separate address books for home and office, and a stamp supply at both locations. This may astonish you (or it may sound all too familiar), but there are people who write notes and never send them, simply because they don't have stamps handy.

Thank-you notes

After all those birthdays, holidays and graduations, your mother probably has you well-trained to write a thank-you note whenever you receive a gift. But when it comes to effective networking, you should look beyond the material gifts you receive and consider less tangible exchanges to be gifts—including referrals, the sharing of information or time, interviews, introductions and even acknowledgments of your achievements. Always respond with your appreciation in the form of an old-fashioned thank-you note. Such as:

Dear Linda,

As I've just returned from a delightful lunch meeting with Tom English, you are on my mind, and I wanted to thank you so much for introducing us at last week's meeting. I've had my eye on Worldwide Widget Inc., for a long time now, and the chance to learn more about the company from an "insider," particularly someone at Tom's level, is meaningful to me indeed.

Again, thank you for your "matchmaking" efforts. And, rest assured, the next time they serve chocolate mousse at our meeting, you'll get mine!

Sincerely,
Laura

Follow-up action regarding a referral warrants another acknowledgment. Say your friend put you in touch with a hiring manager at a growing corporation. You, of course, thanked her when you first touched base and set up the informational interview. But let's say you meet with the manager again, perhaps this time to take a tour of the business. Let your friend know. You don't have to be effusively grateful. Simply inform her of the activity.

Dear Linda,

Just wanted to let you know that I met with Tom—again—yesterday. He offered to give me a tour of Worldwide Widget, Inc., which reaffirmed my high opinions of this fast-growing firm. I also discovered that a woman in my Toastmasters group just started working in the HR department there!

Anyway, I want to thank you again for putting me in touch with Tom. I've enjoyed getting to know him and learning more about WWI.

Warmest regards,
Laura

Send a thank-you when someone's given you some helpful information.

Dear John,

I just mailed off my application for the Self-Employed Communicators Association. Thanks so much for sharing your information on the organization. I had never even heard of it, and what with my sudden need for a good health insurance, this affiliation is invaluable to me. If you hadn't suggested SECA, I'd probably be paying horrendous premiums. Instead, I get a good plan as well as all the other valuable benefits its membership offers.
Thanks again, and I look forward to seeing you soon.

Sincerely,
Sandy

Of course, there are other ways to thank a contact, but none of them replace the thank-you note. However, if you want to further emphasize your appreciation, send flowers, food or candy, invite your contact to lunch or offer tickets to an event that you know he or she will enjoy.

Lunching

These days, the "let's do lunch" can be extended to having breakfast, coffee or even high tea. Sharing food is an important ritual in the world of business. And no matter what the context of the luncheon is—an informational interview, a request for a referral, a special thank-you or an organized networking function—the rules of etiquette always apply.

The basic ground rule for business luncheons (breakfasts or dinners) is that the person who suggests the lunch is the host. In most cases, this means the host pays the tab. An exception to this would be a lunch shared by long-standing pals who meet regularly. Such rendezvous are nice because you can establish your own custom, either splitting the bill or taking turns picking up the tab. Another exception is lunch with federal government employees, who are required to pay for themselves. Your kind attempt to host actually compromises them, so let it go.

When you're the host

When you act as the host, you must follow through with all the responsibilities. This includes suggesting the place and agenda. You should politely ask about dietary restrictions. For example, you could ask, "Is there anything you prefer not to eat or any place you prefer not to go?" Though it's polite to ask if there are such restrictions, it's impolite to inquire about the reason for the restriction. Your guest's reasons may be religious, moral or health-related, or he or she may not like garlic. In any event, it's none of your business. You should simply make sure the appointed restaurant can accommodate any restrictions, and make a reservation if possible.

Remember, even though you have an agenda, a meal is a social occasion. It's a time to touch base with each other and get to know one another better. Personal conversation is warranted. Focus on listening; don't corner your guest so quickly with your issues that he or she feels put on the spot. You should avoid interrogating your guest; let him or her get a bite in edgewise.

Should you have dessert and coffee? The host takes the lead on this. When your waiter comes by to ask about dessert, ask your guest if he or she has time, and be sensitive to the response. If he or she mentioned an early afternoon meeting during the course of lunch, or seems distracted and keeps looking at his or her watch, ask for the bill. If things seem to be going well, encourage a coffee or dessert.

As for alcohol, a good rule of thumb is to avoid bringing it into the picture. A lot has changed since the days of the two-martini lunch. Many companies have policies that prohibit the consumption of alcohol during business hours. However, if your guest orders a drink, then it's okay for you to have one as well (provided you aren't prohibited by your company from doing so). Just don't initiate the order.

On the subject of payment, the accepted etiquette is that the host pays the bill. If the purpose of the luncheon is to investigate or conduct business between your company and the guest, then the company you represent is understood to be the host, and your guest is unlikely to insist upon paying or sharing the bill.

If you're going to encounter awkwardness over the bill, it's more likely to happen when the purpose of the luncheon is of a more personal benefit to you—such as an informational interview or a search for a referral. It may be especially thorny if your guest is male and is uncomfortable with allowing a woman to pay. But be assured, there is nothing improper about a woman hosting a man for a business lunch, in which case etiquette *requires* her to pay.

In both situations, try to make advance arrangements for the bill to be brought to you, rather than having the waiter lay it in the middle of the table, or worse, handing it over to your male guest. Even with this advance preparation, your guest (male or female) may make efforts to pay or split the bill, or even to pay the tip. (Some of us feel more comfortable if we at least offer to pay, regardless of who asked whom.) If you maintain your self-confidence at this point, you should be able to wrest away the responsibility. A smooth way to handle this is to smile and say, "No, I asked you," "It's my pleasure." or even "I'll let you get it next time."

When you're the guest

When you are the guest, reason and etiquette dictate that you steer a middle course. For instance, just because someone else is paying doesn't mean it's time to order the most expensive item on the menu, along with an appetizer, drinks and dessert. On the other hand, you shouldn't embarrass your host by merely ordering a side salad and a glass of water.

The proper strategy is to allow the host to take the lead. If your host is familiar with the restaurant and you aren't, ask what he or she likes from the menu. Regarding alcohol, the same rules apply as if you were the host. On the subject of dessert and coffee, your host should offer the decision to you first, and there's nothing improper about making your desires known, whether you need to get back to work, want to indulge in cheesecake or you would like to continue to talk but prefer not to eat dessert.

Assume that your host plans to pay the bill. However, if you sense that there's an awkwardness, graciously offer to split it. And don't forget to say thank you. Hopefully, you've encouraged your host by expressing your appreciation during the meal. (For example: "My, this Moroccan steak salad is delicious. How did you hear about this restaurant?") Regardless of any thanks you may have expressed earlier, conclude your meeting by thanking your host.

When there's no host or guest

Hopefully, when no one is acting as host or guest, you and your lunch partners have developed your own routine for paying the bill. The overriding concept will be a finding a shared concept of fairness, whether you spend tedious minutes breaking the bill down, or just divide the total cost equally (not worrying about who ordered the extra side of guacamole). Be sure to offer your fair share—and don't forget tax and the tip, especially if you leave early. At one time or another, all of us have gotten stuck covering for those who slipped out early and left just enough to cover their tab.

Telephone contact

The first and most important rule for using the phone in business is that your call must have a clearly defined purpose. Business and follow-up calls fall into this category naturally. Trying to keep in touch is an acceptable use of the phone, but the "What's up?" approach isn't advisable. Try to frame your call around some business-related information you want to share, whether it's bumping into a mutual acquaintance, spreading the news about an important conference or congratulating your contact on a new contract she landed.

On the receiving end, the number one rule is to return phone calls! Unless you're out of town, you should return calls within 24 hours. If you are out of the office for a day or more, your voice message should relay the information that you will be out until a specified date. If you work from home, you may have safety concerns about letting others know you are gone for an extended period. If this is the case, devise a way to get the messages (buy an answering machines with remote access or have a trusted neighbor check your messages). Another option is to invest in a voice mail service with a message that clearly does not emanate from your home.

If there's one thing you definitely want to avoid in telephone communications it's playing phone tag. In this day and age it's possible to have a running dialogue with an individual without ever talking directly to him or her. If you're the one seeking a favor, information or a lead—especially if the person you're contacting doesn't know you—leave a message in which you assume responsibility for contact rather than making the other person "it." Identify yourself, give a *brief* explanation of why you're calling and then explain that you'll try again. Leave your number so that the person can call you back if he or she chooses, but make it clear you will keep trying to reach him or her. If this is a long-distance exchange, you must assume the cost of the call along with the responsibility for the contact.

Other telephone etiquette rules:

- Don't leave long messages. State the purpose of your call, but do it briefly.
- If you have call-waiting, turn it off during business hours. Better yet, invest in voice mail. There's nothing more irritating than being put on hold while your caller finds out if someone more important is trying to get in touch.

- When you reach your contact, always ask, "Is this a good time to call?"
- If you're calling based on a referral, you should identify yourself and the mutual contact who referred you immediately.

Keep in mind that networking etiquette is a *subset* of general business etiquette. Rules that apply to networking relationships may change when you're doing business with one another. One good example of this is voice mail. If you are trying to reach someone for a purpose that benefits you but is outside the contact's business, the message you leave should be brief. If, however, you're doing business with the person, the rule may change. It may be best to let the person know exactly why you're calling and what it is that you need, allowing him or her to make better use of time. Be sensitive to your contact's needs, and you'll make the proper judgment.

Conclusion

Knowing and following norms of etiquette is much more than the right or even civil thing to do. In today's world, the smart woman who is a model of good etiquette has an instant advantage in business and social situations. Perhaps she can't impress people with her important job title, impeccable wardrobe, high-powered contacts or long list of important civic involvements. But if she consistently conducts herself with dignity and treats others with courtesy and respect, the playing field is significantly leveled. Why? Because people recognize that such behavior is something you can't buy or manufacture. It's something you're motivated to do, either out of genuine respect for others, or because you set a high standard for yourself—or both.

Part 3

Networking in the corporate world

Chapter 10

Cracking a new corporate order

When I graduated college, I took it for granted that I'd get a job in my field and that, with my share of dues-paying hard work, I'd keep it. So when I quit a good job with a pension plan to move to San Francisco where I had not the slightest employment prospect, I wasn't too worried. Based on my reality to date, I was positive it would only be a matter of time until I had another good job.

In fact, I did land a job within two months of my arrival. But just nine months after I started, the company was sold and my position evaporated overnight. After five long and disconcerting months, I landed a job with a prosperous software company. It was acquired just six months later. While I managed to hang onto my job, I was merged into a culture that was completely at odds with my values. Since I left to become a freelance writer four years ago, I've watched my former company struggle through numerous reorganizations like so many other companies now in the process of finding their competitive equilibrium. Three CEOs, one acquisition and a corporate split later, many employees aren't sure who they should report to.

Would knowing what I was headed for have clipped my wings early on? I don't know. But my days of winging it are over. I wouldn't make a move these days, especially a life-changing cross-country relocation, without first arming myself with all of the information, advice, support and referrals a good network can provide.

—J

On average, a Fortune 150 company will completely reorganize every 14 months. Front-page news of buyouts and mergers is so common that it's easy to believe there will be about six mega-mega-mega corporations left at the end of this century. A modern-day list of corporate anachronisms is sure to include the following: pension, executive track, even "permanent employee" in some companies.

Like a kid entering puberty, the corporate world will never be the same. But instead of raging hormones, advances in technology have thrown the system out of whack. Having to compete in a new global arena has made it gawky and insecure. If it survives the metamorphosis, perhaps a rational, productive (and more adult) corporate model will emerge bearing little resemblance to the awkward, unpredictable stand-in that's presently wreaking havoc. But in the meantime, the process of "maturing"—through downsizing and rightsizing and restructuring—is going to be painful.

Wouldn't you know it? Just as we women have established a presence on the venerable corporate ladder, it folds. Well, good riddance to the ladder. Because the irony is that in the process of fighting to squeeze into the male model for executive success, we have forged a pretty efficient model of our own: the network.

All for one, one for all

"Because of networking, we've become players," Geraldine Ferraro, a former New York representative to Congress and the first woman vice-presidential candidate on a national party ticket, told members of the National Association for Female Executives (NAFE) members at its May 1995 Satellite Conference.

She speaks from experience, of course. When Ferraro got her start, there were very few female role models in the Queens (New York) District Attorney's Office. What's more, she and other women lawyers were repeatedly shut out of the process of nominating judicial candidates. "We said 'enough,' " she remembered. She and her colleagues banded together to set rules for a separate and independent review of judicial candidates—and then published their evaluations. The attention they got earned them some clout.

Over the years, our relationships with other women have become valuable currency. But after a generation of "party-crashing," corporate women are still limited when it comes to calling the shots. Just how far have we gotten now that the corporate ladder has started to wobble?

We've come a long way—but we're not there yet

If sheer numbers were a measure of our status, we could say we've "arrived." Women comprise a majority of the nation's population and 46 percent of the total labor force.

The glass ceiling. Only 5 percent of all working women occupy top executive-level jobs and 40 percent of Fortune 1000 corporate boards still don't have even one women director.

Still, the glass ceiling has risen over the years. Today it floats at different levels in different organizations and industries. For example, women hold only about 16 percent of management positions in manufacturing compared to 38 percent in services and 41 percent in financial services, according to *Industry Week*.

But glass walls also bar some women from opportunities because they have family obligations and glass doors bar others from meaningful entry into traditionally male-dominated fields and institutions. Who can forget Shannon Faulkner's unwelcome and short-lived admission to The Citadel?

Cents on the dollar. While most families need two incomes to survive these days, the average woman earns approximately 70 cents for every dollar earned by a man—30 percent less pay over the course of a career can result in not purchasing a house or providing a college education. It can prove devastating for families with single mothers. Women are sole breadwinners in a quarter to a third of the world's families.

The family penalty. Married or not, working women tend to be the primary caretakers for their families—which can make their careers vulnerable. Only a small number of companies offer "family friendly" benefits and flexible schedules. Mothers, especially those who work outside regular 9 to 5 hours, often struggle to find regular affordable child care.

For some women, caring for a family can become a natural barrier to advancement. Wives and mothers are not as free to relocate to take advantage of better opportunities. Studies have shown that just the perception that women are bound by family commitments may cause their companies to avoid offering them the opportunities they need to advance.

Influence (back)peddling. In 1994, only 13 percent of the experts and sources quoted in business magazines and newspapers were women. Despite an increase in the number of powerful female role models, such as First Lady Hillary Rodham Clinton, lack of self-esteem lags accomplishment for many women.

"In my eight years with this organization, I have heard hundreds of women say, apologetically, 'I'm not sure that I should belong to NAFE. I'm not a real executive,' " writes Wendy Reid Crisp, executive director of NAFE, in the organization's *Executive Female* magazine. "What must a person accomplish before she is considered—or considers herself—real?"

From boot camp to born leader

Clearly there is a lot that needs changing. But after spending all these years trying to correctly salute the traditional corporate military model, our time may have arrived.

The qualities women bring to business are a perfect fit for the requirements of the new corporate model. We are virtuosos at building relationships and productive alliances. We are flexible enough to lead diverse teams and comfortable shepherding people through the disruption of ongoing reorganizations. From this perspective, the world of work offers women an abundance of opportunities.

Smaller companies. The real growth in employment and an abundance of leadership opportunities can be found in smaller and smaller firms. Fast-track companies may operate with little or no administrative support. Women are practiced at forging connections that result in working smarter.

Teams. Department borders are blurring in favor of multidisciplinary teams that come together for a brief time to tackle a particular project. These teams need leaders who are committed to smoothing the way to a productive conclusion, even if that means rolling up their sleeves and working side by side with team members.

International alliances. Multicultural differences have been instrumental in redefining business as usual. In a global community, international alliances are necessary for survival and overseas assignments are becoming an increasingly common corporate right of passage. Yet corporate executives are finding that most productive alliances must begin with relationships. While women are still a rare breed overseas (comprising only about 12 percent of the expatriate population in 1994), those who are sensitive to such relationships are bound to fare better than their male counterparts.

Networking: There *is* security out there

While all of this flux is stirring up some changes that promise to be positive for women, it has taken away a lot of the security we've come to expect. From one day to the next, we've got to be prepared to turn on a dime. There are fewer promises and more things to know. Most of us will change jobs sooner than we change cars. At a time when we can no longer owe our loyalty to any one company, our networks are a long-term resource we can turn to again and again throughout our entire career for:

Information. There's no trick to finding information these days. There is enough to bury the average seeker. The key is to be able sort through the overload. In the chapters ahead, you'll find out how your network can help you learn what you need to know to shine in your next job interview or make a career transition. After you've landed a job, you'll see how a network can help you work more productively and stay abreast of new trends in your industry.

Support. Relationships are the currency of a new corporate order. Without them, you would never be able to handle an overload of work in the midst of staff cuts or negotiate the emotional ups and downs of a career. In the pages ahead, you'll meet women who have forged strategic alliances to help them build influence at all levels of their organizations. Others have created mentoring relationships that pave the way for women on the way up.

Exposure. Whether you're going after your first job or your next promotion, getting noticed is integral to your career. In the beginning, networking can bring you face to face with the people who can support you, hire you and promote you. With time it will provide a forum for displaying leadership skills.

Referrals. You never know when you'll need your next job. When that time comes, cover letters and resumes don't hold a candle to personal referrals. People simply feel more comfortable hiring someone who comes highly recommended. Networking can provide a synergy—helping you develop the new skills and achieve the visibility and contacts in one job that can open to door to the next.

The company you keep

"By sharing gender, we share common needs," Geraldine Ferraro told the NAFE Satellite Conference attendees. "Building on our commonalities can make it easier for us all."

It's also safe to say that our needs as individuals and as a group will continue to change in unexpected ways, so the more multidimensional our networks, the more prepared we will be to meet each new opportunity. In the chapters head, you'll meet women in the process of defining their careers by the company they keep.

Chapter 11

Getting a job (and keeping it)

If you're currently looking for a job, could you use some inside information about a company you think you'd like to work for? How about the name of someone who is currently hiring in your field?

Who wouldn't? In fact, it's pretty safe to say that if you *don't* have this kind of an edge in today's intensely competitive market, you can expect to be beat out time and again by other people who do. The world has changed a bit since recruiters flocked to college campuses to woo new graduates and jobs were lifetime commitments. Now getting a job is not your only priority. You're also likely to spend a few sleepless nights worrying about keeping it in the midst of rampant downsizings and reorganizations.

All of this makes having a network you can call upon for information, support and referrals more essential than ever before. After all, not every interview turns into a job. But every network connection has the potential to reshape your destiny.

Facing down Catch-22, -23 and -24

Generations of new college graduates have experienced a variation of the no-win situation popularized in Joseph Heller's novel entitled *Catch-22*: They can't get a job without experience, and they can't get experience without, you guessed it...

These days, though, it's much tougher than it's ever been for newly minted graduates to get a first job. At least 20 percent will finally settle for positions that don't require a college education, according the U.S. Bureau of Labor Statistics.

Add to this another perennial that we'll call "Catch-23": Roughly 80 percent of all available jobs are never advertised in the classified ads or reported in trade journals. Personal, often informal, connections have always opened more doors than any cover letter or college degree.

And just when you land a job and start thinking that it's safe to relax, "Catch-24" rears its head. No matter how welcome you feel today, there is no guarantee you'll be toasting marshmallows at next year's company picnic. No hard feelings. It's the nature of a new world of work.

Playing by new rules

"You can't assume your employer will take care of you forever," says U.S. Secretary of Labor, Richard Reich. "The old rules (of career advancement) don't apply anymore. You have to learn the new rules." But just what are these new rules?

Rule #1. You're in charge. Meet the boss: She's you. You may not have your sights set on a management position, but you will be very much in the business of managing your own career from day one. If you wait for your company to escort you down that path of regular reviews (you know, the ones that lead to regular promotions), you may find yourself waiting in line for an unemployment check before you realize what happened.

Companies simply aren't making any promises to their employees anymore. Yet they are expecting more. So if you want to advance, you will have to keep one eye on your performance (in terms of "What value am I contributing to the company?") and the other on your options and new opportunities to move your career in the direction you've chosen. Fortunately you don't have to go it alone.

Rule #2. You're not in unless you're plugged in. It doesn't pay to keep your head down and your nose to the grindstone these days. There is too much going on around you that can affect your future. Out of sight and out of mind can eventually mean you're out of a job. Because you can't be everywhere at once or find out everything you need to know on your own, your network is a lifeline. As you'll see, it can not only help you get a foot in the door of the company you'd like to work for, but secure your future prospects.

Networking strategies: getting a job

Networking adds a synergy to your job-seeking efforts. In the process of making new contacts and gathering information, you are planting the seeds that ensure you won't have to work so hard next time.

How to get the information you need

When you're looking for a job, you need a lot of information. Which companies are hiring? What kind of jobs are available? To cinch the interview you should be prepared to talk about the issues facing the company and industry. Contrary to what you may be feeling, the goal should *not* be to snap up your first offer. It should be to hire yourself the best company. By planting yourself in the right soil, you'll have a better chance of succeeding (i.e., keeping the job you get, which, incidentally, is the subject of the second half of this chapter.) So how to do you learn what you need to know?

Take a course. In answer to an uncertain environment, there are an abundance of workshops, seminars and courses available for job seekers at all levels and in all predicaments. Many seminars offered through career resource centers and outplacement services are not only ideal places to find job leads and learn skills that can give you an advantage during the hiring process, but many make networking a structured part of the program.

After three years in publishing, Angelina Beitia, vice president and director of circulation for *Macworld* magazine, attended the publishing course sponsored by Radcliffe College. "A major focus of the course was getting to know people in the industry," she says. Each night industry professionals talked with the class of 60 students (a valuable network in itself) about what they did and how they got to where they were. "In many ways it was staged networking," says Beitia. "I don't necessarily think it's how it's done in the real world, but I think if you're just starting out and aren't dialed in yet, going to staged networking events can be a really great opportunity to meet people in industry."

Go online. Some career development experts predict that within five years, online services will become the most prevalent means of nonlocal hiring and recruitment. A flickering screen instead of a human face? We don't like to focus on any interaction that doesn't involve face-to-face contact, but this resource cannot be overlooked as a convenient and relatively economical way to locate (and be located by) companies and recruiters who are hiring.

There are currently a multitude of electronic job-search services specifically geared to matching prospective candidates with companies that are hiring. Services such as Adnet, kiNexus and Job Bank USA contain job listings posted by employers that job seekers can respond to online or via regular mail. Some play matchmaker, actively matching the resumes or career profiles of job seekers with available openings posted by their client companies.

By subscribing to an electronic job search service, "you, in effect, are networking 24 hours a day, seven days a week, 365 days a year," say Ronald L. and Caryl Rae Krannich, authors of *The New NetWork Your Way to Job and Career Success*. They also encourage job seekers to continue to update their posted resumes even while they are happily employed.

Overall an estimated 50 to 80 percent of the jobs are technical, but that is changing. More than 30 percent of the jobs listed by companies like Kraft and General Foods on Online Career Center, a nonprofit national recruiting service serving more than 3,000 companies on the World Wide Web, are in sales and marketing and health care.

Career resources are available via the Internet, the World Wide Web (the graphical portion of the Internet) as well as local services and commercial on-line services, such as America Online and CompuServe. Private companies, universities, associations and even outplacement services have all gotten into the act, as well. Some recruiters regularly "drop in" on online forums to seek out qualified people.

In addition to job listings, job seekers can track down sometimes obscure information to impress a prospective employer in an interview, or "chat" with someone who can provide inside information about an industry or employer. Specialized women's services, such as Women's Wire, even provide online career coaching.

The best news is that these resources probably won't leave you too much out-of-pocket. In fact, many online services are free to job hunters who want to post resumes and browse listings. Spending an hour or so a day researching companies and chatting with others on the Internet or a commercial service can cost you $20 to $40 per month. (For addresses of online services, see the resources section of this book.)

Tap your organization's job bank. Announcements about available jobs are a standard part of the meeting agenda for most networking organizations. Many organizations, such as Women in Communications, Inc. (WICI), also list available jobs in their newsletters and sponsor free job "hotlines" with recorded information about jobs posted by area employers who are interested in reaching the organization's diverse professional membership.

Conduct an informational interview. So often job seekers become paralyzed because nothing seems to be happening (no one is calling for an interview). Interviewing for information only is a great way to begin making something happen.

Once the pressure to hire you is off, most people are genuinely willing to spend some time with you, sharing information and offering you the kind of feedback that can help you sit head and shoulders taller than another candidate when you get to the interview hot seat. Are you presenting the right image? Are you light in some areas of knowledge? Is there anyone else you should talk to? This is the time to find out.

"Several times a year people send me a resume and ask for 10 minutes of my time," says Angelina Beitia, who points out that even if there is no job open, making the personal connection is well worth the time and effort. "If you get in front of people who don't know you, they *will* know you by the time you leave," she says. "When (a colleague) calls me for a referral, I can yank out the resume and say, 'Here's somebody for you.' "

How to get the support you need

Join or form a support group. It's tough out there. Sometimes it helps to know somebody else is going through the same struggles you are.

Large companies are bringing in outplacement services or establishing in-house resource centers for people who have been laid off or want to research career transitions. Community career resource centers offer regular career counseling sessions. In these settings, informal support groups can easily flourish. Members can benefit by comparing notes about trials and patting each other on the back for triumphs.

"I didn't happen to know anyone else who was out of work at the time I was," says Ginny Reed, who used the resources of Career Action Center, Palo Alto, California. "I was up there every morning in their Job Search Group. We'd sit around and talk about the things we'd done and the things we needed and share ideas with each another. I had the feeling that I had some friends who were going through the same thing I was going through."

Of course, a support group can also grow out of an informal gathering of friends or former colleagues who have lived through a layoff together. But to prevent your meetings from turning into gab-fests or gripe sessions, some career experts suggest going a step further to assemble a group of people who will not only agree to follow your progress but hold you accountable for making a certain number of contacts a day or week.

It's wisest to choose people who have your best interests at heart, but who can be objective enough to give you practical guidance on issues such as whether or not to accept a particular job offer. (Former bosses and professors are two good choices.)

How to get the exposure you need

Get actively involved. The key word is "active." Join an organization and volunteer to write an article for the newsletter or sit on a committee. People will quickly get to know you through your contributions. When a job opportunity arises that you're suited for, your name is more likely to come up.

While this kind of exposure can result in a referral within a short period of time, it is just as likely to pay dividends later on. In this market, that's like money in the bank.

Playing a leadership role in her industry's association placed Pamela Mills in the spotlight. While she was happily employed managing a college bookstore in Colorado Springs, she was recommended for a job at Iowa State University by a member of her association who'd been impressed with her commitment and drive.

Get a temporary foot in the door. With many companies opting for "contingency" workers over permanent employees, temporary services firms have become booming businesses. Since you're likely to have time on your hands (and no doubt be in need of funds) while you're job hunting, a temporary assignment may turn out to be the foot in the door you need.

About 38 percent of temps are offered jobs as a result of an assignment. Again, the exposure factor is working in your favor. And if the offer isn't forthcoming, you will have an ideal opportunity to add important connections to your network. Just be sure to keep in touch. Even if your temporary supervisor doesn't have the authority to hire, he or she may be able to pass along some information about other openings—as well as a recommendation.

Make friends in low places. In a recent survey of 150 executives, 60 percent said their assistant's opinion about the job candidate was "very" or "somewhat" important. Make it a priority to record and remember the names of secretaries, interviewers and anyone else involved with your job search. Send them a personal thank-you note afterward and be sure to follow up periodically. These people may be able to give you valuable leads.

How to get the referrals you need

Ask for them. The beauty of having a diverse network is that everyone you know will be at different stages of career development with something different to share. When Susan Hailey was preparing to embark on the search that landed her in her current job, she turned to a former summer intern who had graduated from her business school. "He'd gone through a job search and found a job, so I called him and said, "John, I'm thinking about doing a job search. Do you have any suggestions?" she says. "He sent me probably two inches of information he had collected, including an alumni job posting bulletin that had this job in it. He couldn't have been more generous. Even after I came to work here, he called me two or three more times about jobs he found and said, 'You'd be perfect for this.' I said 'John, I got the job,' " she laughs.

Networking strategies: keeping your job

You may have landed a great job, but this is no time to check your networking skills at the door. You must be ever-vigilant that your job is continuing to contribute real value to your company's future success. Your network can help you improve your skills, cultivate support among your colleagues and bring you visibility. If you've taken a job in sales or marketing, networking to get quality referrals will become part of your everyday life.

How to get the information you need

Create a brain trust. Now that your career is cooking, you want to keep it on course. It's never too early to identify a group of people who can become resources for the information and advice you need to manage your career. Although you probably won't meet formally as a group, your personal "board of directors"—made up of colleagues, peers and professional contacts—will be available to guide you in assessing corporate politics or streamlining your department's budget, for example.

How to get the support you need

Draft a mentor. If you're lucky, you'll have more than one mentor over the course of your career. (For more detailed information on the process of choosing a mentor, see Chapter 4.) A few hundred companies and organizations offer structured mentoring programs for women. Some pair a mentor and protégé according to the goals of the protégé. Others are designed to foster leadership skills.

At Hewlett-Packard, mentoring is one component of the Leadership Effectiveness and Development program (LEAD). The program was originally targeted at the company's field sales force. However, based on its overwhelming success, it has been rolled out to other organizations within the company.

A shortage of female role models promoted J.C. Penney Company executives to create a continuing leadership forum featuring speeches by noteworthy women "until we grew our own role models," explains Gail Duff-Bloom, senior executive vice president and director of personnel and company communications. Now 300 mentors help their protégés expand their knowledge, enhance their management skills and learn to work together more effectively. A similar program called the "Buddy System" serves administrative people.

Since 1990, the Philadelphia Women's Network (PWN) has sponsored Career Wise, a program that pairs mentors and protégés based on the protégé's goals for career improvement. Matches are made on the basis of extensive interviews. Because PWN requires members to have nine years of combined college-level education plus work experience, the protégés are often women who have not yet met the membership requirements, but who are interested in growing into future members of the organization.

How to get the exposure you need

Build an internal network. According to Sue Gould, a career counselor and performance coach, this is a critical part of a two-part networking strategy. "How are you going to be on the front burner when it comes to promotions and new opportunities if you're not present in peoples' minds?" she says. But there is an even more practical aspect to having an internal network. "You may not always have the authority to accomplish something in an organization." "A lot of times you have to accomplish things through informal influence. If you have a strong and active network, it's a lot easier to work with people up and down the ladder. Some of the most important people in an organization are the administrative assistants and the executive secretaries. They're the gatekeepers. If you don't build a relationship with these people, it can become very difficult to get in to see their bosses."

Make connections with individuals at all levels of the company—whether it's taking the receptionist to lunch on occasion or working on a task force with your peers in another department. These relationships could prove invaluable.

Build an external network. But there must be a balance. And for some people, Part 2 is just as hard to manage as Part 1 is for others. "There's so much to do in your job and your personal life that you forget about how important it is to stay in touch with what's going on out there," Gould acknowledges. But even if you aren't courting a job change, "People not directly tied to your day-to-day job may be able to provide what I call 'field information' you can use in your job."

You can't seem to find time in your busy schedule to attend networking events or meetings of professional or community groups? Think about it. "There are lots of times when you can be hooking into your network or renewing old network contacts and expanding it too," Gould tells her clients. "Once people begin to focus in on that, they begin to realize that they do have time for breakfast or lunch or a drink after work."

Speak up. Many of us are still struggling with being Ms. Nice Girl. But as much as the idea of broadcasting your accomplishments chafes, you must. You can't expect your superiors (the very people who might tomorrow decide to include you in a downsizing) to automatically know how valuable you are. You have to tell them in so many words. Talk about your successes, giving credit where credit is due, of course. Take part in industry conferences and share your knowledge in memos or multi-department meetings. Speaking up may be your best opportunity to purchase security.

How to get the referrals you need

Maybe you're already thinking about your next job. If you've taken pains to cultivate a rich network, it will serve you well. But if you're in sales, referrals mean customers—your bread and butter. For you, part employee, part entrepreneur—networking is a way of life.

Get it down cold. "Cold calling is the start of networking." insists Lollie Moyer. As a recruiter, she says matching people to jobs is very much like connecting the dots. "You call one person and they say, 'Gosh, I don't have anything, but one of my counterparts in Louisiana has an opening, why don't you give her a call...?' Pretty soon that thread leads you along a path." Although Moyer can count on a network of contacts she's established after many years in the business, she admits that cold calling the contacts given to her by her network is still part of her repertoire. "I can sit down with five names and by the end of the evening I have 25."

Become an insider. To prevent yourself from not becoming the "unknown bidder," you must find a way to gain access to someone on the inside of your prospective customer's company." While you may never be able to speak to the ultimate decision-maker, you may be able to gain influence by using information your network can provide.

A consultant may be able to clarify the approval or recommendation process or give you feedback on your proposal. If you have genuine concerns about aspects of the project before you submit your proposal, you may be able to get a face-to-face meeting with its authors.

Conclusion: Keep in touch

Perhaps you've networked your way into a situation you wouldn't think of leaving in the foreseeable future. Congratulations! But that doesn't mean you need your network any less.

"My advice is to take all calls and return all calls," says Susan Hailey. "Make yourself available. Do what you can to make sure you connect. Because I think what happens is that you make yourself available and in turn you plant the seeds from which things will grow that you can benefit from."

Chapter 12

Advancing toward
your goals

You're running...running...effortlessly. Up ahead, you can see the executive suite glimmering seductively, finally within reach. You begin to pull ahead...but wait! You stop short, teetering on the edge of a sheer drop-off, your heart pounding. The next ledge—the one that appeared so accessible just a moment ago—is still there. But now you realize it's much too far away for you to survive the leap...

Bad dream? These days, many middle managers who thought they were poised to move ahead are waking up to find there is nowhere to go. There are very few neatly manicured career paths leading directly into upper management anymore. Even the garden-variety promotion—the kind that used to bring additional money and status—is not the given it once was. Many managers wonder if they will ever make a vertical move again.

As women, we can guess what all this will mean for us. In spite of the fact that we've watched more women make the impossible leap into the executive suite in recent years, most of us will be left with all of the old barriers to breaking through that glass ceiling—as well as the prospect of watching our careers go as flat as the new corporate model.

Then again, we may able to move more efficiently on flat land than we could within the traditional hierarchy. The new team ethic that has replaced the familiar system of management-by-entitlement is based on creating relationships. Leadership is required instead of delegation and supervision: pulling a diverse group of professionals into a cohesive project team, parceling project work out to independent contractors, shepherding people through a minefield of reorganizations and rightsizings.

We should rejoice. Finally the corporate world wants the stuff women are naturally good at. According to Carolyn S. Duff and Barbara Cohen, authors of *When Women Work Together*, "Whether that old-boy system continues to hold us back in the new workplace depends on how strong an old-girl system we can create."

We may not be calling ourselves "old girls" just yet, but it's clear that our networks have already primed us to succeed in a cooperative environment. In this chapter, you'll find out how to use a web of connections to extend your influence inside your company and position yourself to advance in the direction of your career goals.

Despite the gusto that women have shown in blazing a trail into the corporate world, and despite the fact that firms that have good glass-ceiling records tend to outperform firms that don't, experts puzzle that our numbers drop off sharply at the highest levels of management.

Progress continues to be slow. Of the 70 new women who joined Fortune 1000 boards in 1994, more than half were first-time board members. Directorship, a firm that maintains a carefully screened list of candidates (one-third of them women) for executive positions, reports a "significant" increase in the number of their client companies targeting women to fill top spots.

So what's holding us back?

The majority of women still face some pretty formidable barriers to achieving influence equal to a man's.

The status quo. Resistance to change seems to get stronger as the air gets thinner. Way up in the boardroom, there's often little incentive for members of the back-slapping men's club to change their ways to accommodate women who have "made it." As a result, these pioneers often end up feeling isolated and reluctant to be too outspoken about women's issues. A 1992 Center for Creative Leadership study confirms that both female and male executives see a sense of intense scrutiny as a major barrier to women's advancement.

Ourselves. Surprise! This is a complicated issue that may be rooted in our own unconscious loyalty to business as usual. In trying to measure ourselves against a system designed for men, some women respond to the gap between their styles and the "norm" by developing a lack of self-esteem.

"Traditionally it has been believed that women managers do not see themselves as positively as men," says Lawrence A. Pfaff in *Executive Woman* magazine. According to a survey conducted by his human resources consulting firm, supervisors and employees both rated the performance of women managers higher than the women rated themselves.

The promotion penalty. Throughout the 30 years since the Equal Pay Act was born, courts have had trouble understanding the distinction between job titles and responsibilities at the management level. As a result of many rulings, jobs that require similar levels of skill, effort and responsibility are unevenly compensated, more so at higher levels than low. The salary gap between women and men in administrative support jobs is 25 percent, but jumps to 35 percent for administrative, managerial and executive positions.

That old double standard. A new study shows that women's chances of getting ahead are slimmer than their male peers' simply because they don't get as many opportunities to prove their mettle.

Based on more than 500 responses from managers in five corporations and one government agency, the Center for Creative Leadership study found that women are often overlooked when key assignments with international responsibilities and intense external pressure open up. The perception among many men doling out the assignments seems to be that women with family obligations will not be able carry their weight in certain situations. One thing is certain: Without the opportunity to try, women will forfeit the promotions.

How to get the information you need

Find a tutor. Keeping your knowledge and skills up to date is essential if you plan on moving ahead. But since you won't be able to pop out to a seminar every time you need to know something new, it's a good idea to find someone with whom you can exchange expertise. Depending on what you need to learn, your tutor may be a peer in another department or organization or even another industry.

Hire only the best and brightest. Another twist is to hire yourself an assistant-cum-tutor. Junior people are often younger and much more familiar with cutting edge innovations in technology, for example. Having one of the best and brightest as a member of your team will help you keep your skills toned and marketable, says Sue Gould, a career counselor and performance coach.

How to get the support you need

Get a career coach. Careers are more complicated in the '90s, especially for women managers trying to balance the fast track with home and family roles. A career coach (professional or informal) can help you sort it all out—whether you feel like you're in over your head or simply need a reality check.

Professional coaches can be pricey, but they may be well worth the investment if you are having trouble moving ahead. An experienced coach, as opposed to a casual buddy, will be able to detect chinks in your armor that may be hindering your image or performance. Together you can implement a strategy to counteract your failings. Another time a coach can prove invaluable is when you're actively considering your next career move.

"There's nobody here who's really appropriate for me to have that conversation with," says Susan Hailey, director of business development and planning for Resumix, a Silicon Valley software firm. When she sits down with Sue Gould, a career counselor and performance coach, Hailey says she is free to explore tricky topics like salary negotiation. "I'm at a level now that I need to be able to do that well. It's really nice to be able to role-play with somebody," she says.

Partner with a peer. Of course, sometimes you simply need the same kind of inspiration a sports coach would give his or her players: "Get out there and push harder!" An informal contact who doesn't work with you can also become an ideal sounding board.

Sandra Borrer-Jury, a Philadelphia-based consultant, found this kind of support in a "peer-partnering" relationship. "In my previous position, I was the only female among my peers," she says. "The other women in my office belonged to the clerical staff, so I didn't feel I had anybody to bounce ideas off of or talk to in confidence about some of the concerns that I had."

Support your staff. Influence-building begins in your own department. If you genuinely support the professional growth and career advancement of each member of your staff, they, in turn, will support you.

In addition to mobilizing the resources they need to do their jobs, listen to their ideas, encourage them to become more visible in the company by offering support to other departments and advertise their individual and collective achievements to upper management and colleagues in other departments. Not only will you be underlining your department's value in the scheme of the company's future but you may have a much better chance of attracting the best people to your team.

One woman I worked for loved to go on about how she much she "empowered" her staff. The fact is that most of the time, she played the part of a remote generalissimo. When she did walk among the masses, she might dispense praise that usually sounded as superficial as a sound bite. But just as often she was critical and overly blunt.

Eventually, this otherwise bright and accomplished woman turned her department into an enemy camp. She spent a great deal of time campaigning for the political affections of people above her or at the same level on the organizational totem pole. Meanwhile the people who worked for her resisted going the extra mile and avoided giving her meaningful feedback.

By all other accounts, this manager seemed poised to move up. Except that while she was out polishing her professional credentials, she was earning a reputation as someone who "should not be in a position to manage other people." As a result it took several years and a lot of maneuvering for her to negotiate the move she had in mind.

—J

Make collaborators of your colleagues. The people whose compliance and cooperation you depend on are critical to your success. By making allies of your peers, even those who at first appear to be adversaries, you can ensure a steady flow of information and resources that allows you to handle more work—even during staff cuts or other shakeups. In addition to getting the job done, you are extending your influence.

How to get the exposure you need

Register your expertise. If sitting on a board of directors is part of your career plan, you can boost your visibility by getting your name on a local or national placement database. These databases "formalize a way for women to rub shoulders with top management," Kaye O'Riordan, corporate secretary of the grocery chain Albertson's, said in an interview in *Working Woman* magazine. Albertson's recently used a corporate-board placement service that contains the names of about 1,800 women, administered by Catalyst, a women's research organization, to locate a second woman for its board.

Similarly, registries organized by women's commissions, have long helped place women on state boards, task forces and commissions. California State Senator Lucy Killea recently sponsored legislation to set up the first government-run database of women candidates for corporate board seats. Intended primarily for Californians but also open to out-of-staters, the database received more than 400 requests for applications before they were even printed!

An invitation to the executive suite may be easier to come by if you enhance your corporate leadership capabilities with service on a board of directors for a national industry organization, high-profile service or nonprofit group. Begin by volunteering for committees. As you become more visible, you will gain the support you need to throw your hat into the ring.

Turn to your network to put women in power. Funny how time flies. The support group you formed when you were just starting out years ago may now be full of senior managers. That's what happened to one Boston area women's networking group. After meeting monthly for seven years, the members of self-proclaimed A-Team realized by 1981, "We were all working for new CEOs. We could have been the CEOs," Elaine Ullian said in an *Executive Woman* profile.

As a group, they went out to make it happen. At the time only one of the more than 60 hospitals in the Boston area was run by a female executive. On the advice of a headhunter who specialized in the health care field, A-Team members added their names to CEO recruitment lists. Then, every time they heard of an opening for a CEO of a hospital in the area, group members called their contacts at other city hospitals to recommend fellow A-Team members for the post. Within about five years, close to half the members of the network of 12 to 15 women occupied top executive positions.

Make international contacts. More and more, a stint abroad is becoming a prerequisite for moving into top management. Though women are still underrepresented, women's networks are making it easier to forge international connections through alliances with affiliate groups around the world.

For example, the International Professional Network (INET), a NAFE affiliate in Tel Aviv, Israel, provides reciprocal benefits and an open invitation to American NAFE members who wish to attend meetings while visiting in Israel.

Brush up on your golf game. Of course, you'll be able to hob nob with executives at conferences and industry cocktail parties, but there's no more fertile ground for high-level networking than a fairway. Yet only about a quarter as many women as men play golf according to a 1993 study by the National Golf Foundation.

It wouldn't hurt to brush up on your game. The Ladies Professional Golf Association (LPGA) recently presented a clinic sponsored by The Gillette Co., in which about 200 San Francisco Bay Area businesswomen got pointers on the game of golf—as well as the more difficult game of making points with boss.

How to get the referrals you need

Check out job candidates. At this stage of your career, you'll probably tap into your network as much to check out prospective new hires as prospective jobs. "My network provides a very good reality check on the reputation of a candidate at a higher level," says Angelina Beitia, vice president and director of circulation for *Macworld* magazine. "Of course, you can't raid your network, but references are easy to get. And I trust the opinions of the people in my network."

Reconnect. If you're planning a major change, however, it helps to cast what is probably already a rich network farther and wider. The more people you can connect and reconnect with, the better the field of opportunities you'll be able to survey. Hidden pockets can be gold mines. "If you've taken any kind of professional program or gone to undergraduate or graduate school, you also have this network out there," reminds Sue Gould. "Among all of these people, there are probably more than a few who are doing similar things all over the country, maybe all over the world. You're bound to hear about different opportunities in other organizations. If nothing else, they can help you see what's coming down the pike."

Conclusion

As your career matures, inevitably so do your networking skills. "I've gotten more selective," says Susan Hailey. "I used to be naive enough to think that I had to call the highest-level person I could possibly call to find out about an opportunity—even if I didn't know the person, even if I had to find a way to engineer an introduction. I've learned that that isn't always necessary. It's much better to contact people who you feel comfortable with. I think what happens is that as you get more focused in your career, you begin to have a better sense for what makes sense for you."

Chapter 13

Reinventing
your career

Just as she was beginning to burn out on teaching, Ginny Reed decided to go to summer school. As a computer buff, she had gotten to be a pro at helping other teachers use the resident Apple computer to maintain students' grades. So when one of her colleagues who ran the summer youth employment program asked if she'd like to lend her expertise, she said yes. "At the end of the summer, I was talking with another teacher and he gave me the name of someone at Apple. I called her and wound up getting an interview," Reed says. Today, she tests software for Apple Computer.

"I really don't want to leave my job," says Angelina Beitia, vice president and director of circulation for *Macworld* magazine in San Francisco. So when her husband took a job in Salt Lake City, she decided to give telecommuting a try. She'll spend two days a week working from her new home in Salt Lake City and three days working in the magazine's offices. "I think it can work short-term," she says, admitting, "I don't know whether that's going to be a year or two years or three years." That poses a question: Shouldn't she start looking for a job in Salt Lake City just in case? "Even if I decide to pursue a job there, my network is here. I'll have to create a new network," she says. "It's going to be very interesting."

And so it is for many women these days.

An unpredictable corporate climate, family obligations and even lack of personal satisfaction can dictate fundamental changes in any chosen career path. By choice or by chance, you may find yourself reinventing your life's work more than once—whether that means transferring your skills to a more economically viable career, creating a flexible work schedule or going back to school.

As women, we tend to be more "at risk" for encountering some changes, such as integrating a spouse's geographical move into our own career plans. But we may also be more *open* to change. According to the U.S. Bureau of

Labor Statistics, the average woman over the age 25 changes jobs every 4.8 years (compared with 6.6 years for men).

Career experts note that while men tend to talk to executive recruiters when they want to make a change, women talk to other women. Our networks are giving us the power to capitalize on the many options not readily available a decade or two ago—and perhaps the freedom to create a few of our own opportunities.

Can't get no satisfaction?

All the buzz about "reinventing" yourself seems to have more to do with making sure you survive the next downsizing than anything else. But the fact is that many women are choosing to reinvent or simply restyle their careers for reasons other than merely staying in the game. We are more inclined to view dissatisfaction as a temporary setback than merely an unhappy fact of life. Many of us feel a need to redefine success. That can mean anything from creating a better balance between work and family to rethinking a career choice.

A recent survey of nearly 2,000 Americans found that only 30 percent of the working women who responded are happy with the ratio of work and home time in their lives. A third of the working mothers responding to another survey said they would choose to work only part-time if finances were not a consideration.

Most startling to experts is a new trend among middle-aged women (35 to 49 years of age) who have, by most accounts, "made it." When *Fortune* magazine surveyed 300 women (nearly all of whom were managers and executives) 87 percent said they had made or were seriously considering making a major change in their lives. About 45 percent said they had started their own business or changed jobs or were seriously considering doing so. Nearly 40 percent said they had gone back to school or taken a sabbatical or were seriously thinking about it.

While change can be uncomfortable, the alternative may be worse. Nursing a case of dissatisfaction on the job these days will almost surely be rewarded by a layoff or a poor reference somewhere down the line.

Networking along the path less traveled

No one will be able to hand you a trusty map at a crossroads in your career. The beauty of networking is that it provides precisely the guidance and support you need at every step—even if you start out not knowing where you're headed.

Reassess

Any career move should begin as a self-assessment. What are your marketable strengths and achievements? What other jobs require the same qualities and skills?

The day she was laid off from her full-time job as a technical support liaison for Chevron Corporation was "the saddest day of my life," remembers Elena Gaoiran. "I didn't know what I was going to do with myself in my late 40s." Using her company's career placement resources, she began to focus on identifying her transferable skills while she networked with other "displaced" professionals. Over time, she was able to see how her gift for working with many different kinds of personalities to resolve problems, along with her broad knowledge of the information technology function within a major corporation, could help her get into technical recruiting.

At this stage you may opt to work closely with a career counselor or job placement service. (By all means, add these new contacts to your expanding network!) But don't discount network connections from your "former" life. They can help you identify qualities you may be overlooking or taking for granted.

Explore the possibilities

Now, what are your options? Through your network contacts, you may discover you're wearing blinders that are limiting your view. For example, you may learn you really don't have to go back to school to get a job in another industry. Or you can hang onto your manager status and still work part-time. Networking can bring you into contact with a variety of people who can give you the real lowdown about what they do for a living. If nothing else, they will help you rule out a lot of potential options.

Try something out

At some point, the pieces will begin to fall into place. A recruiter who spoke about the satisfaction she got from helping people find jobs "planted the seed in my mind," Gaoiran remembers. "The next time I saw her at a job fair. I told her 'I want a job like yours.' Once I was able to verbalize it, it took off."

As you zero in on your new goal, your network contacts can supply inside information that will help you build confidence and possibly get a foot in the door. "I'd go to networking meetings and tell people I was looking for a position as a technical recruiter. One day, somebody said, 'I saw something on the bulletin board you should check out,' " Gaoiran says.

Regroup and refine

Even a foot in the door can result in a minor misstep. It's all part of the process that will lead you to your ultimate goal. Gaoiran's initial foray into recruiting proved to be a commission sales position. "Financially I couldn't handle it," she says. "I also found out a few things about myself. I didn't like working at home. I learned I really need to be with people."

But she found the short-term experience went a long way toward helping her shift gears. "My six months as an account manager gave me just enough background to start interviewing for a staff position. When I went in to interview, I could go in as a recruiter," she says.

Of course, being plugged into a diverse network will make it that much easier to correct your course. Whether you're making a minor career transition or a major life change, your network can provide you with a never-ending supply of information, support, exposure and, ultimately, referrals.

How to get the information you need

Find a mentor—or become one. A mentor can provide the focused guidance that can help you move ahead in a chosen career. So when your choices change, you are likely to need different sources of expertise. (See Chapter 4 for how to find a mentor.)

But if you don't yet have a focus, and are chafing in your present situation, you may bc able to learn more by mentoring someone else.

After mentoring a young woman who was determined to break out of the administrative ranks into marketing, Sandra Borrer-Jury says, "I learned that I had more to offer than I thought I did. I was in a position that I wasn't that crazy about, so while I was helping her evaluate her career skills and rework her resume, I did a lot of self-evaluation, too. It was motivational."

In examining your transferable skills, you may not give yourself credit for knowing things not bestowed to you by a formal degree or title. Then working as a financial analyst, Borrer-Jury lacked hands-on management experience. "I found that you don't really have to have management experience to be able to offer good advice," she says. "In talking to my protégé about my experience, I found I was mixing a little bit of political advice with career development advice."

Become resourceful. Attending professional conferences, seminars sponsored by outplacement services or adult education courses in your new area of interest will give you important information that will help you feel like an insider. Once you understand the ins and outs, key trends and key players, you'll feel confident enough to approach new contacts who can advance your exploration to the next level.

Go online. Specialized bulletin boards and online "chat" groups can also provide an introduction to lingo and issues important in your new area of interest. Start by being a fly on the wall and just listen in to discussions. In time, you'll grow bold enough to speak up and forge connections with others who are already doing what you want to do.

Interview—for information only. First-time job hunters know that this can be a great way to find out enough about a prospective job or situation to embrace it—or eliminate it as a possibility. When you're seeking a career transition, it is especially important to poke around for holes in your current knowledge. ("Could I substitute experience for training or special credentials?") Informational interviews can also bring you one step closer to an interview. ("Are there any particular companies or people who you think I should contact?")

How to get the support you need

Partner with a peer. The magnitude of the change you're making will determine whether you need the guidance of a *bona fide* mentor or whether a peer working in another job or industry might be able to fill in a few gaps.

"It's more like sharing," says Sandra Borrer-Jury, who has acted as both a mentor and a peer partner. "You're both pretty much on the same level, you both have experience, but there's something you need that you can't get from close friends or the people you work with." Many people enter this type of relationship with a specific goal in mind, such as learning more about public relations or finance, for example.

If you stay within a large company with a policy for transferring managers, cultivating geographically diverse peers can be a good move. For Gail Duff-Bloom, senior vice president and director of personnel and company communications, rising through the ranks of J.C. Penney Company meant that she was often relocated to departments throughout the country. With each move, "My networking contacts acted as a safety net when I left my comfort zone," she told the NAFE Satellite Conference attendees.

Turn to a support group. Making a change can be an emotional process. When everything seems to be in a state of flux, there is nothing more welcome than a familiar shoulder to cry on. If you're afraid of making a change, an informal support group can be the best place to talk about your fears with other women you trust.

Members of some groups help each other remain poised to take advantage of change. "We call ourselves the Incredibly Intelligent Women's Group," says Susan Hailey, director of business development and planning for Resumix, a software company. A group of her former co-workers have continued meeting regularly throughout the years. Building on that bond, they have decided to help enlighten each other about current topics—such as what's happening on the Internet. By group decree, one member prepares a topic to present for each meeting and then the group discusses it.

Enlist the help of male colleagues. The higher you rise, the more likely you are to encounter resistance from male incumbents. Unfortunately in the context of the old-boy network, the more a woman speaks out for women issues, the more resistance she is likely to encounter. The solution? Try to enlist a well-regarded "inside man"—in other words, a male colleague—as an advocate, says Judith Mueller in *Executive Female* magazine. Mueller is the executive director of the Women's Center, a career-development organization in Vienna, Virginia. You can begin by discussing issues that concern you with a male colleague you trust and respect. According to Mueller, you might say "I've noticed how well you handle some of the problem-solving that we do, and how fair you are." While she admits this can be a slow process, Mueller insists that people—men included—like to be seen as agents of change.

Form—or reform—your advisory board. If you've taken our advice in previous chapters, you may already have a working advisory board whose collective feedback has helped you set priorities and manage your progress. Now that you're thinking about making a career change, it may be time to add a few new "heads"—*director of career transitions*, for example, or *senior vice president of geographical transfers*.

These new advisers may be people you know well or individuals you'd like to know better. "Aside from advising you, they can also do some matchmaking that might eventually result in getting your dream job," says Joyce A. Schwarz, a career counselor and author of *Successful Recareering*.

How to get the exposure you need

Move in the right circles. It may be that simply increasing your involvement in your current organization will give you the additional skills you need to make a career transition. But if you're changing the course of your career, chances are that your networking affiliations should also change to reflect your new goals. By now you know that there are a multitude of networking groups and organizations—many with very specialized goals. By visiting prospective new groups (most groups invite a prospective member to attend meetings as a guest before joining), you can determine which groups are most appropriate for the new you.

Don't be surprised if you find that what's appropriate now is actually worlds away from what you planned at the start of your career. "I never thought in a million years I'd be joining the Junior League," says Angelina Beitia. "But it's the only organization I know of in Salt Lake City for non-Mormon businesswomen."

Two words of caution: First, don't throw out the old in favor of the new, if for no other reason than that you enjoy and gain support from the continued connection. After she was laid off from her job, Elena Gaoiran broadened her connections to include NAFE and the San Francisco Commonwealth Club in anticipation of making a needed career change. But one membership she was determined to hang onto was her membership with the Chevron Women's Golf Club. "I still look forward to playing golf with my former co-workers," she says.

Secondly, try not to overextend yourself. "When I moved to the Philadelphia area eight years ago, I didn't know a soul," says Sandra Borrer-Jury. "I immediately joined everything I possibly could—Junior League, my neighborhood association, my alumni chapter out here. It all came to a head about a year and half ago. I was on overload." Since then, she's been letting some memberships go, and focusing more of her energies on increasing her involvement in organizations that have consistently proven valuable.

How to get the referrals you need

Talk about your plans. Tell your story (just don't go on and on) to people you meet at industry meetings, seminars and cocktail parties. These are the people who have the information and resources you need to accelerate your career change. Even if they are not active matchmakers, most people make mental connections that often lead to physical contacts.

Act on cue. There are many things you can share with the people you've never met, but who can potentially provide referrals that will help you make a transition. Cultivate a peer working in another state. Contact a fellow alumnus of your college or university who works in the industry or city you're targeting. Sometimes a common interest is all it takes to "warm up" an otherwise cold call.

"I went to Harvard Business School so I have access to a huge directory of Harvard alumni who have agreed to be available to help other alumni by telephone or letter," says Susan Hailey. "It's a really good program. I've been called several times myself."

Conclusion

Whether you seek it or it finds you, change can be both an exhilarating and unsettling experience. However, many successful women have taken a decidedly unconventional route to end up where they are, so you will be in good company. With the help of your network, you already are.

Part 4

Networking to build your business

Chapter 14

Women, networking and the small-business revolution

Recently I looked around and was surprised to find that only one of my close female friends still works full-time for a company. Like leaves drifting from an oak, we writers, artists, designers and consultants have gradually let go of the corporate world and landed in our own businesses.

That's not to say it's always been easy. But over the years I've noticed a different tenor in our conversations—even our kvetching. Yes, the marketplace is competitive, and some clients can be beastly. Niggling doubts about the direction we've set for ourselves may keep us awake some nights. But in the end, solutions always seem to emerge that we would have cynically, or wistfully, dismissed over the water cooler. My relationships with other independent women have literally helped me survive and thrive "out here."

Now I realize that we are a microcosm of a much bigger revolution.

—J

By now it's obvious—at times painfully obvious—that major changes are occurring in the shape and structure of American business. The corporate world is running lean and mean, downsizing and outsourcing, shifting and flattening. And jobs are going away—forever.

But American businessmen and women know that where there is change, there is also opportunity, and increasing numbers of them are opening their own small businesses. Powerful, cost-effective technology fuels this small-business renaissance, and women entrepreneurs are right in the thick of it.

If you're already part of the revolution, or you're thinking of joining in, the next few chapters will demonstrate how networking can give you a competitive edge, connecting you with the information and support you need, and creating opportunities for exposure and referrals.

You'll also meet a new breed of businesswoman, one who's unfettered by the traditional rules and structures of doing business in a male-dominated, corporate environment. These women are networking to forge innovative new alliances with organizations, business partners, colleagues, vendors and even competitors. Their experiences will offer a fresh perspective on problems you're likely to encounter at every stage of business development.

But first, let's take a closer look at current business trends and how far women have come.

Flexing our collective muscle

After an epidemic of downsizing, 99 percent of all U.S. companies now meet the government's traditional definition of a "small business," that is, a company with 500 or fewer employees. But if the numbers all indicate that small business is becoming an economic force, to what degree are women taking part in the trend? Women currently own about one-third of all U.S. small businesses, and the number is growing.

Small business means big opportunity for women, despite the fact that the majority of us are starting out with less experience and less than half the capital of our male counterparts, according to the Small Business Administration (SBA). Women are becoming an economic force to be reckoned with, and this translates to the kind of clout that makes government lawmakers begin (however slowly) to take notice. For example:

- For the first time in history, there is a woman at the helm of the House Small Business Committee.
- The SBA has significantly improved access to start-up capital— good news for women who have traditionally run into obstacles finding it. Under a pilot program that prequalifies women business owners for guaranteed loans, the number of loans to women-owned businesses rose from 3,800 in 1993 to 5,400 in 1995.
- The National Women's Business Council is a new federal advisory panel that focuses on promoting changes in policy and legislation to support the growth of women-owned businesses. The council is also committed to increasing access to capital and improving data collection on the economic impact of women-owned businesses.

Women: defying the odds

Who are today's women entrepreneurs? They are former corporate officers who have taken an "early retirement." They are mothers who want to spend more time with their families. They are retirees looking for a way to stay active and supplement a fixed income.

Of course, turning the dream into reality is not without risks, but women seem to be forging ahead despite a number of disadvantages, including:

- **Lack of experience and training.** Studies show that most women start businesses with less experience than men. Low-income women who can't afford training in finance and marketing and other business fundamentals are at an even greater disadvantage.

- **Lack of funding.** "Bootstrapping" has been a necessity for most women entrepreneurs who have traditionally lacked access to start-up (seed) capital. Women receive only 1 percent of venture capital seed money and less than 5 percent of all venture capital. Many banks are still reluctant to make loans to women.

- **Lack of support for family obligations.** Most families need two incomes to survive. Yet women, who often have primary responsibility for caring for their children, have found that flexibility in the corporate world is slow in coming. At the same time, many women are reluctant to give up challenging work and sacrifice years of hard-won professional experience. While working at home won't relieve women of their primary caretaker roles, it may be the only way most can build any kind of flexibility into their lives.

Despite these disadvantages, women are challenging the status quo in pursuit of their dreams.

Home is where the business is

The majority of us start as—and remain, often by choice—sole proprietors, with *home* as the home base for our enterprises. In fact, according to *Home Business News*, women operate two-thirds of the nation's 24 million home-based businesses, and the number of those businesses is rapidly growing. By the end of 1995, 44 percent of all U.S. households will be "in business" at least part of the time, according to BIS Strategic Decisions, a market research firm in Norwell, Massachusetts. With an estimated 8,000 new businesses opening every day, the vast majority of us may be taking our coffee breaks in our slippers before the year 2000, as prophesied 15 years ago by futurist Alvin Toffler in his book, *The Third Wave*.

A new perspective on risk

Perhaps you're excited by this trend toward home-based business and want to try it for yourself. Perhaps you already have. If you've ever researched starting a business, then you're probably aware of the sobering official line on risk: On the average, a mere 20 percent of all new businesses survive their first three years.

However, recent surveys indicate prospects may be much better for *home-based* businesses. (Remember, the majority are run by women.) According to Link Resources, a New York City-based research and consulting firm, 85 percent of the home-based businesses it studied from 1990 through 1992 were still alive at the end of three years. Certainly, lower overhead makes it easier to keep a business—especially a part-time venture—going. But there are other critical factors that contribute to success.

- **Access to resources.** With the clout of a small business "revolution" behind them, entrepreneurs are benefiting from a growing array of resources—from training to financing—many targeted to low-income women. For example, the SBA has launched a new program that should improve access to seed money with a minimum of paperwork. Under the Women's Prequalification Pilot Loan Program, a woman who receives the SBA's approval of her business plan can walk into a bank with a loan guarantee in hand.

- **Resourcefulness.** Years of playing the underdog in the corporate world have given many women a special kind of grit—determination to find a way. In the chapters ahead, you'll meet some of them. Through their experiences you'll discover how your networking connections can help you.

New opportunities

You may choose to work from home (and you may remain sole proprietor of your business), but it isn't necessary—and it may not be wise—to work alone. Women with networking know-how can benefit from business networking opportunities that aren't available to corporate workers. These include:

Virtual organizations. When companies distill their work forces down to a core staff, necessity becomes the mother of invention. According to James Collins, lecturer in entrepreneurship for Stanford University, we'll be seeing more companies made up of networks of people who aren't employees. Inside (and increasingly outside) of companies, "virtual" business structures are taking shape.

Inside a "virtual corporation" sits a core staff who could not run the company without outsourcing work to independent consultants, contractors and freelancers. To handle often complex tasks, many of these independents combine talents to form cooperative "virtual organizations." Within San Francisco's freelance creative community, for example, many creative directors, designers, writers and media people are combining their credentials to form ad hoc "virtual companies."

Multilevel marketing. Because distribution typically takes the biggest bite out of the retail dollar, companies that are positioned to efficiently and economically market their products worldwide will be marked for unparalleled growth, according to Professor Paul Zane Pilzer, economic adviser to presidents Reagan and Bush.

Chief among them are as many as 2,000 multilevel marketing companies, such as Amway and Mary Kay Cosmetics, that currently employ a combined sales force of about 12 million people worldwide.

The premise for multilevel marketing is simple. Independent salespeople (the majority are moonlighters) earn commissions of 30 to 50 percent on product sales. Anyone who recruits new salespeople can move up a level and begin earning a portion of the commissions earned by his or her recruits. When your recruits recruit new people, you're in line for a portion of their earnings as well—with the potential, over time, to earn a six-figure income.

The multilevel structure seems economically fashioned for cooperation: The better your recruits do, the better you do. So, it can literally pay for sales consultants at higher levels of the organization to spend time helping new consultants improve their performance and sales. At Mary Kay Cosmetics, formal and informal networking has become a way of life for many sales consultants.

Little wonder, then, that women account for as much as 90 percent of the front-line sales force in high-profile companies like Mary Kay Cosmetics, Amway, Shaklee and Tupperware. Despite the lingering stigma of "pyramid schemes" (companies that focused on recruiting at the expense of selling products), most well-known multilevel marketing companies have lengthy track records and solid reputations.

And just as different business structures are emerging that suit independent workers, technology and computer communications are shrinking the world and expanding opportunities for small and home-based businesses owners. New opportunities include:

Setting up shop in cyberspace. Although estimates indicate that women constitute a piddling 10 percent of the country's online community, the number of savvy businesswomen conducting and discussing business online is on the rise. (Nearly half of the small-business clients served by America Online are women, according to the founder of the business forum.)

And why not? No one can quibble with the convenience and economy of posting a message on a national electronic bulletin board or greeting thousands of potential customers who browse the Internet's World Wide Web.

1. **Commercial services.** As subscribers to CompuServe, PRODIGY and other services, businesswomen regularly tap into specialized databanks, get feedback and leads from "chatting" in open forums, post information about products and services on bulletin boards and stay in touch with contacts and clients via e-mail.

2. **Specialized services.** There are 67,000 local bulletin boards serving almost 17 million users around the country. Many people believe that these smaller online communities will outlast the impersonal commercial metropolises such as America Online.

3. **The Net.** The Internet's 25,000 networks (including government agencies, educational institutions and private commercial enterprises) simulate a bazaar. In addition, more than 30,000 sites have sprung up on the World Wide Web, the graphical portion of the Internet. While lack of security for online credit card transactions remains an issue, the Web affords businesses of all sizes an opportunity to promote their wares to thousands of users.

Going for the global gusto. Growth in export markets has grown at an average annual rate of 9 percent over the last decade—far better than the average 2.3 percent annual growth in the domestic economy in recent years.

Economists and the U.S. government are betting on export markets to remain healthy over the long haul, and more and more women are expected to take part in this brave new world. U.S. Census figures show that 7.5 percent of all women-owned business reported some share of revenues from exports, compared with 6.1 percent for businesses owned by men. A 1992 survey of about 1,000 members of the National Foundation for Women Business Owners (NFWBO) found that 10.4 percent were involved in exporting and 22 percent were considering getting involved. This comes as no surprise to some of us.

"Successful exporting is based on personal relationships, nurturing contacts over a very long time before you eventually make a sale," said Small

Business Foundation of America executive director Regina Tracy in *Working Woman* magazine. "Women tend to think in terms of relationships like that."

Years ago, I was listening to a boyfriend speak expansively of doing business in the Pacific Rim. He seemed to believe it would require little more than deciding to go for it. Having worked closely with business people in Singapore and Malaysia to launch an international workshop program, I commented that I had learned that the quality of the relationship determines the quality of the business in that part of the world. There was silence. After a few uncomfortable moments, he dropped the subject altogether. I suppose he blamed my muddled feminine thinking. Perhaps he meant to spare me the indignity of explaining that something as warm and fuzzy as a "relationship" had no place in the rough-and-tumble arena he had earned the right to play in.

Since then, new international markets have opened up and the Internet has made businesspeople around the world much more accessible. But one thing remains the same. You need to forge solid relationships to succeed overseas. I hope that, by now, my former friend has learned that information is a precious byproduct of networking. (I often wonder how many lessons he's had to learn the hard way.)

—J

Networking: catalyst and comfort

The irony is that even though most women are sole proprietors of their businesses, going it alone is not a viable option anymore. There's too much to know, too much to do and too much competition out there.

Networking will ultimately bring you word-of-mouth referrals to feed the coffers. In the meantime, the information, support and exposure you receive from your network will provide a catalyst for the referrals you seek. In the following chapters, we'll explore a variety of ways your networking contacts can help you start and grow your business with the benefit of:

Information. When you're in business, what you don't know can do you in. In this high-tech age, access to information is not a problem. The problem is knowing where to look. We'll tell you how to network to find sources of training and information you can use to build and expand your business.

Support. Isolation makes a poor business partner. Your network contacts can lead to informal support groups that can help you improve your creativity while working alone. Or you may form strategic partnerships that can help to accomplish more than you ever could working alone.

Exposure. People want to know you and trust you before they hire you. You'll see that networking offers you many opportunities to demonstrate your expertise and build new skills, whether you're starting out or starting over.

Referrals. The sum of your networking interactions and activities will be word-of-mouth referrals that will build your business—more surely than relying solely on satisfied customers and more cost-effectively than advertising or other tradition promotional efforts.

Conclusion

The good news is that the more time you invest in building and nurturing your network, the greater the payoffs. Networking author Ivan Misner has done the research to prove it.

As part of his doctoral work at the University of Southern California, Misner conducted a study of referral generation among members of Business Network Intl. (BNI). The study showed that the likelihood of receiving 100 or more leads virtually doubles with each year of participation. People who participated for one to two years identified their largest referral to be more than 50 times higher than people who have been members for less than one year.

Misner's study also found that the number of spin-off referrals (referrals generated from referrals) increased with time. He cites the example of a photographer, a BNI member for almost two years, who was referred to a service company. After he completed the job, individual employees of that company called to request family portraits. He eventually returned to photograph the company's annual awards banquet. All told, one referral was worth almost $10,000 in spin-off business.

We hope you're convinced. Now, let's take a closer look at how networking can help you give your new business wings.

Chapter 15

Giving your new business wings

When I met an alumnus of my university for lunch one cold, rainy after-noon, I was between jobs. She, fresh from a successful career as an editor at a major woman's magazine in New York City, was freelancing full-time. At the time, I was doing some freelance work, too, to make ends meet. Even though I had dreamed of living her life, I couldn't really see myself doing it. There were all kinds of roadblocks, real and imagined, in my way.

After learning a little about my background and experience, she re-marked, very matter-of-factly, "You could be doing this right now if you wanted to."

It may not seem exactly earth-shattering in the telling, but in that mo-ment, she succeeded in opening a window in my doubts. While it took three more years for me to finally make the break, from that day on I understood that I was the only one standing in the way of making my dream a reality.

I also learned never to underestimate the power of support—given and received. It's as much a component of your success as your most loyal client.

—J

If you're reading this chapter, you're likely to feel that working for your-self beats working for a corporation. For many of us, independence is its own reward, not to mention the fact that the corporate environment no longer offers career safety. At a time when new economic growth is coming from outside established companies, there may be more security in working for yourself and serving many clients.

That said, most of us start out in business ready to take on the world, only to find that the world isn't inclined to cooperate. Our best-laid plans spring a leak when we least expect it. We are blind-sided by the isolation of running a home-based business. Leads suddenly dry up. If there's one thing we can be sure of, the unexpected will happen.

It's reassuring to know that, in nearly every instance, networking connections can fill the gap—with information, support and resources. In this chapter, we look at a variety of services, programs, technologies and opportunities that are available to you as a small-company or home-based businesswoman.

Through these organizations, services, technologies and techniques, you may learn how to write a business plan, gain access to start-up capital, receive free individual business consulting, find emotional support for making it through the first shaky months, increase your visibility and get referrals. But to make the most of any of these opportunities, you'll need to use your networking skills, and if you do, you'll be rewarded with knowledge, support and business growth.

Sources of information

You can't get by on your professional expertise and hard work alone. Glossing over market research or neglecting to plan cash flow can cripple—or kill—even the best business, let alone a new one. When you're the one wearing all the hats, you'll significantly improve your chances of succeeding by understanding basic business operations, including finance and marketing.

Here are some ideas for getting involved with organizations, development programs and online services that offer information, training and a wealth of networking opportunities for new entrepreneurs.

Enroll in a microenterprise development program. If you wouldn't know a business plan from a diet plan, this is the place to start. Often aligned with local economic development programs, microenterprise development centers offer training and support—and often sliding price scales for low- and moderate-income women and minorities.

One such program is the Women's Initiative for Self-Employment (WISE) in San Francisco. Graduates of WISE business planning courses may use their completed business plans to apply for a WISE loan of up to $5,000. "Loans are made based on a person's ability to run the business, not on her credit record," says Tomoko Lipp, an instructor and administrative consultant to WISE. Like many other microenterprise programs, WISE has also forged relationships with local lenders to give graduates additional sources of seed money.

But not everything is budgets and bottom lines. Networking happens spontaneously through the intensive training program, as well as in industry-based "action groups." "I encourage participants to exchange information," Lipp says. "Even people who are just starting a business have a lot of good information in the form of research."

Join a knowledge network. While large national groups such as Women in Communications, Inc. (WICI) and the National Association for Female Executives (NAFE) tend to offer support on general business and career issues, many are also sponsoring smaller specialized groups, such as roundtables, speakerships and forums, to enlighten and train entrepreneurs with specific needs.

When I started pricing my freelance writing services, the feedback I received informally from friends in the business was that I was charging too little. Because I didn't have a clear idea of what professionals with comparable experience were charging, I was at a disadvantage.

At a meeting of a speaker series for freelance writers and designers, I got my answer. A range of sample projects was presented, and our price quotes were recorded. Then a panel of clients told us what they would pay a freelancer to work on the same projects. It was eye-opening to say the least. And the value of the information I got that evening can be quantified in dollars and cents!

—J

With the support of NAFE, Thérèse Watley started the Home-Based Entrepreneur Network (HEN) to give other women like herself a place to exchange ideas, resources and experiences. The 30-plus members own businesses that offer a range of products and services—from gift baskets to medical billing. "A lot of our members are in the start-up stages, so they need information about how to structure their businesses, where to go for financing and how to select the best business courses," she says. Each month a guest speaker addresses one of these topics of interest.

There are a number of similar "special focus networks" among the 200 grass roots groups sponsored by NAFE, says Melissa Wahl, senior manager of network services. Any member who wants to start a local group is welcome to send NAFE information about her idea.

NAFE is prepared to assist by helping chairpersons of new special focus networks find other NAFE members who are willing to get involved. NAFE then offers coaching and provides materials and support to make it easier for the new groups to grow.

"It doesn't matter to us whether someone is a secretary or the president of a company," Wahl says. "We're looking for people who genuinely want to have regular opportunities to present programs, exchange information and provide an environment that will promote professional development and personal growth."

Contact the Small Business Administration (SBA). A number of new initiatives under the Clinton Administration have pumped new vitality into the SBA. For one thing, staffing has increased by 5 percent in local offices, where most new and prospective entrepreneurs are likely to show up for training, free one-on-one counseling and assistance with the issues that arise when starting a new business.

SBA counseling programs are not set up for one-time visits. This makes your local SBA office fertile ground for networking with other entrepreneurs. In addition, each district office has a women's business representative to assist you with small-business questions and to distribute information on upcoming events in your area.

The majority of SBA-sponsored training and counseling is conducted through its three largest resources.

- **The Service Corps of Retired Executives (SCORE).** This army of 12,000 retired business professionals can lend you the benefit of an average 35 years of business experience. In addition to their free one-on-one counseling sessions, they conduct low-cost workshops on a variety of business-related subjects.

- **Small Business Institutes (SBIs).** Here you can receive intensive management counseling from graduate and undergraduate business students working under expert faculty guidance. This includes a report and oral presentation detailing the actions you need to take to improve your business operations. (Contact your local SBA district office to learn how to contact the nearest SBI school.)

- **Small Business Development Centers (SBDCs).** Typically located on college and university campuses, more than 750 SBDC offices nationwide offer counseling, training and research assistance covering all aspects of business management, including finance, marketing, production, organization and technical problems.

In addition to these services, the SBA offers a broad spectrum of special financing programs, workshops and conferences that target groups such as women, minorities and veterans who face special challenges. These range from "Meet the Lender" courses on financing to free business opportunity conferences for displaced military personnel and small businesses struggling in communities affected by defense downsizing.

If you live in Seattle, Houston, Atlanta, St. Louis, Boston, Kansas City, Chicago or Los Angeles, you can also visit an SBA-sponsored Business Information Center (BIC). In addition to one-on-one counseling, BICs provide computer databases, videotapes, reference material, software applications, tutorials and interactive media as well as resources to help you determine your start-up needs.

Prospect for local resources. Begin by asking the chamber of commerce or your local economic development office for a complete listing of the small-business resources available in your community. Also consult the yellow pages, free business publications and resource directories. You might be pleasantly surprised at how many resources—ranging from nonprofit resource centers to business start-up kits—you're able to dig up right in your own backyard. Many chambers of commerce offer small-business roundtables and other specialized groups designed to bring local entrepreneurs together.

Venture online. Even before you open your doors, you can be scouting for information—and potential clients—online. Here's an overview of what's available:

- **Commercial services.** Services such as CompuServe, GEnie, America Online, PRODIGY and Delphi offer specialized bulletin boards that can yield everything from technical information for resolving a computer glitch to a field-tested marketing idea from a bona fide business expert.

  For example, CompuServe puts you in touch with small-business gurus Paul and Sarah Edwards via The Working From Home forum. GEnie hosts The Home Office/Small Business RoundTable, as well as more specialized Work at Home, Self-Employment and Small Business Advertising and Marketing forums. Delphi offers you the opportunity to host your own custom forum to a specialized group or market.

- **Specialized services.** According to some, as more people get their feet wet using expansive (but impersonal) commercial services, more will seek out or return to specialized services.

  "It's just a different forum in which a networking exchange can take place," explains Evelyn English, who founded and chairs the Westchester Women in Business Network. Instead of gathering in one spot to listen to a speaker once a month, members network exclusively online, downloading the content of a presentation to read at their convenience. The topic remains "open" for about a month, so that members can post their questions or comment in the conference area of the bulletin board or e-mail each other. The beauty of this approach, English says, is that members retain more of the information because they have an opportunity to digest and discuss it over the course of a month.

- **The Net.** Ready for the Big Kahuna? In this vast "virtual community," you'll find UseNet discussion groups on every topic known to woman. By subscribing to (e-mail) mailing lists, you'll automatically receive every message posted to the list (or selected messages if the group is moderated by an actual human being). By the same token, you can post a query and essentially poll a broad, international audience representing your peers and potential customers.

  You'll also find the World Wide Web, the graphical portion of the Net, where one of these days you may set up a virtual storefront to attract a worldwide audience.

- **Uncle Sam Online.** The SBA provides toll-free access to online tutorials, SBA publications, calendars of local events, as well as information on SBA programs for women, minorities and veterans. E-mail forums encourage networking among small-business owners. There's also a gateway to more than 60 other federal online services.

Sources of support

You may have been raring to go in the beginning, but after only a few months as a "solo" proprietor, you find you miss your office chums. The distraction-free environment you took pride in creating has turned into an isolation chamber. You're surprised at how emotionally vulnerable you feel.

Even the most competent and motivated of us can buckle under the stress of handling everything alone. Networking offers a number of ways to enlist many different types of support you'll need. Some of the possibilities follow.

Turn to a business incubator. Maybe running a business from your spare bedroom is not an option—or even a desire. Research shows that you may be giving your newborn business a better chance of survival by starting it in a business incubator.

The nation's 600 or so business incubators offer new entrepreneurs inexpensive office space bundled with a range of support services such as accounting, legal and marketing advice. Survival prospects tend to be much better than average: Research shows that more than 80 percent of small businesses that spend two or three years in an incubator are still in operation, with many of them increasing revenues and creating jobs. And the networking opportunities can be amazing.

According to Michel Perdreau, director of member services for the National Business Incubation Association (NBIA), incubators may choose to foster economically disadvantaged groups, specialty businesses (such as food) or they may serve whole communities, representing businesses in areas as diverse as manufacturing and fine arts.

More than half of NBIA member incubators are in urban areas. The remainder can be found in rural areas (28 percent) and suburban areas (19 percent). Almost half are sponsored by government and nonprofit organizations to promote economic development. Incubators may also be affiliated with universities and colleges, or sponsored by arts organizations, church groups and chambers of commerce. A growing segment of these incubators are cosponsored by large private sector firms such as Corning and Digital Equipment Corporation.

If family or finances keep you working at home, you may be able to take advantage of an affiliate program offered by some incubators. This includes a package of services, ranging from financial counseling to e-mail, usually for a fee below market rate. And of course, you will have plenty of opportunities to network with other fledgling entrepreneurs.

Join a barter network. When you're just starting out, cash can be tight. Why not trade your expertise or products for the office supplies or car repairs you need to ease your business through a cash crunch? Bartering may also turn into a great way to build a client base.

While members of your core network can become your barter buddies, you might also consider signing on with a formal barter exchange. In 1994, barter transactions in North America totaled $7.6 billion according the International Reciprocal Trade Association.

Joining one of 600 barter networks is better than taking out an ad in the yellow pages. For an annual cost ranging from $100 to $600, you get a brief description of your products or services listed in the network's catalog. Most networks then charge a commission (10 to 15 percent of the value of the transaction). It may be split equally between the buyer and the seller.

Form an informal support group. "I never would have started my business if I didn't have other women supporting me, giving me advice and saying, 'I know it's tough. I do it too,' " admits Laura Gates.

While part of her plan for launching her public relations and marketing firm involved networking for referrals through a variety of formal organizations, Gates also started a small, private business support group.

By limiting its membership to fewer than 10 people, the group can address the problems of each individual and brainstorm together to help solve them. "We made a commitment to each other that everything that goes on in the room is confidential. We've really gotten to know each other and can talk about our problems," she says.

The group has taken on the dynamic character of the people in it. "The first year we spent most of our time griping about how to get business and about all the rules and regulations and detail of running an office. Now we're griping about how to handle and control the growth," she adds.

Sources of exposure

Exposure has a chilly sound—like you're "out there" all alone. Perhaps you panic at the thought of injecting yourself into a group discussion or volunteering to co-chair a community fund raiser. But if you have a little faith, your courage will bring an important reward: Visibility.

The fact is, most people will want to know you—and more importantly trust you—before they feel comfortable hiring your company. Scratch the polished surface of an experienced networker and you're likely to find someone who pales at the prospect of mingling with a group of new people. Just knowing that helps. So let's start with some true confessions.

"Basically I'm an introvert," confides Andra Brack, executive director of the Indiana region of Business Network Intl. (BNI). Yet she consistently gives the appearance of someone who is self-assured. She regularly speaks before groups of professionals and advises, praises and encourages members of BNI. She points to her own experiences as evidence that networking can be learned. "It's independent of personality or field. It is more of an attitude," she says.

While Laura Gates encourages her female clients of public relations and marketing firms to "get out there," she concedes it isn't any easier for her than it is for them. "Before I had my business, it was hard for me to just walk right up to people and talk to them," she admits. "It's still hard, but now I use my business as a way of getting to know people. If I hear people talking about business, it's easier to use my business as an entree into the conversation. I just say something like, 'Oh, I had a client who did that.' It's sort of like my business is my front," she says.

One way to make it easier on yourself is to reach out to someone else who appears to be having the same feelings. "Whenever I go into a new setting, I try to find someone who looks a little more uncomfortable than I do," says writer Betsy Brill. "It's taken years for me to be able to just take a deep breath and go in and introduce myself. But now I go ahead and barrel forward."

Choose the right environment. Like a company's underlying culture, a networking organization's philosophy, values and atmosphere will ultimately determine whether you flourish there.

Feeling comfortable talking with other members should be an important part of your criteria for selecting organizations as you build your network. It's important, therefore, to visit many groups—and several times—even if you're not a "joiner." In fact, it's especially important if you're not a "joiner," because the more you visit, the greater your chances of finding a good fit.

You may find, like many women we interviewed, that you are more comfortable with a less structured forum. Or you may find you welcome a focused approach used by many formal leads groups. One important note: If you're interested in becoming a member of a leads group, be sure you understand the level of commitment that will be expected of you. Some groups have a rather lengthy list of rules for members. BNI groups, for example, frown on members joining other, similar groups and allow a limited number of absences.

Get involved in your community. "The kind of networking I've done is to roll up my sleeves and get involved. I've found it's the most powerful way to make an impact," says Brill. "When you work with other people, they come to trust you and develop confidence in you. That's the best recommendation."

You won't lack opportunities. Almost every nonprofit or community organization is hungry for talent, even raw talent. Introduce yourself to officers, staff and other members. Write articles for the newsletter. Give presentations in your area of expertise. Join the committee or board of a community agency. And treat your volunteer work the same as you would treat a paying job for a high-profile client, because it *is* just as important. That means doing what you say you're going to do when you say you're going to do it, even if a paying job comes up that competes for your time and attention. "You can't just drop the ball," says Brill. "You made a commitment to someone, and they're relying on it as if they're paying." Similarly, if you do a poor job, you'll be nixed from any possible job referrals and become known in the wrong way.

Of course, you need to keep in mind that the wrong kind of exposure can be deadly. Know that one unfortunate gaffe could cost you business—or worse, irreparably damage your professional reputation. In one of her columns, Bernadette Grey, editor-in-chief of *Home Office Computing* magazine, related the story of the owner of a small advertising agency who, during a casual conversation with a local merchant, let it be known that he and his wife always beat the Christmas rush by ordering exclusively from catalogs.

What was wrong with this? On the other side of the conversation was a struggling local merchant. Not only did the advertising agency lose a potential customer, the miffed merchant told the story to several other store owners—also unlikely to be future customers of this advertising agency.

How to get the referrals you need

Now that you're gaining visibility, what are you going to do with it? Don't assume everybody you're networking with knows what you do just because you're in the group or the same business. Even after you get to know someone well, she may not be able to articulate what makes you unique if you haven't done it for her. And if she's not aware of the special service you provide, don't count on her hiring you.

As we've emphasized throughout the book, an important part of the networking process—particularly if you want to attract referrals—is to help people help you. Tell people who you are and what you're looking for. "You really need to know what you want from people," says Laura Gates. "If you don't ask for it, they're not going to know what to give you."

The first thing to do is to get clear on what you do. One way to help others understand and remember your business is to develop a brief, but memorable description of what you do—preferably using 10 words or less. It's not as easy as it sounds, but the point is to clarify your purpose so that you can express it in potential networking situations.

"You want someone to say, 'Tell me more,' " explains Gates. "When I first started out, I said: 'We tell women's success stories.' When you say that, people tend to ask, 'Well what do you mean?' Then it's easy to engage them in a conversation."

What makes you unique? Identify benefits you offer that distinguish you from the competition. Write down your message and be sure to practice it on other people. Ivan Misner, author of *The World's Best Kept Marketing Secret*, suggests using a "memory hook," a phrase that vividly describes what you do. This is especially important if your business is complex. In his book,

Misner tells the story of a man who explained his business effectively by say-ing this to a networking group: "The next time you're in someone's office, look at their telephone system. If they have a phone system with fat wires, they need me."

If your business is more mainstream, you may want to add a little drama. A photographer introducing her business to a networking group might start out by saying, "Have you ever wanted to shoot a relative?" And tailor your message to meet the needs of different types of prospective customers. This will help you target your discussion to areas of interest to your prospective customers.

When business is slow, say so. "There's often a tendency when business is slow not to tell people, because you always want to present the appearance that everything's great," says Betsy Brill. "I've learned to say, 'Well, I was really going great guns there for a while. Now I'm sort of staring at the door wondering what's going to happen next.' A designer I know recently told me that December and January were just like death. She mentioned it to someone else at a networking meeting who said 'You ought to talk with so-and-so, I think there's some design work she needs to have done.' The designer says she's been so busy since then that she can scarcely handle it."

Give away leads. Get in the habit of finding opportunities to give away quality referrals. If you're busy and can't take on a project, congratulate your-self and refer the business to someone else in your group.

"Whatever you take from the group, you have to be willing to give back. You have to try to work within the group before you go outside," says Thérèse Watley, founder of the Home-Based Entrepreneur Network (HEN). This is a rule for many groups.

Give away gifts. Many networking groups have a table on which mem-bers can display their business cards, brochures and work samples. But if your business produces or markets tangible items, don't miss the opportunity to give them away at meetings.

One member of HEN whose business is specialty advertising regularly distributes incentive gifts she handles, such as colored pens. Not only is she a big hit at meetings, she says she's tripled her business since she started focus-ing on networking.

Give it time. "In the work that I do, nothing is a quickie relationship," says Lya Sorano, an international business consultant who founded the At-lanta Business Women's Network. "The clients I worked with in 1994 were people I had been in contact with for an average of 14 and a half months. So the idea that you come to a networking meeting and all of sudden there's a $100,000 job...that does just not exist. People should come with the expectation that they need to build a relationship and that over time things will come from that relationship."

Conclusion

Starting your own business can be both an exhilarating and scary experience. The demands of owning a business will force you to grow and develop as a person and as a professional. It takes a tremendous amount of time and energy, and it means exposing you to a variety of risks. Networking can get you started, help you through the rough spots and expand your opportunities. So stay in touch with your network, and remember to give back as often as you can. You never know what you might need as you enter the second level—growing your business.

Chapter 16

Growing your business

After months of hard work and nail-biting, you wake up one morning and realize you have more work than you can handle. You've not only survived, but despite the inevitable feasts and famines, you're doing fine. If you have more than a moment to contemplate your blessings, you next thought is likely to be, "Now what?"

Is it time to move out of your home office? Hire employees? Upgrade to more powerful technology? Target new markets? Expand your product line? Suddenly, struggling to survive seems like a day at the beach.

Go! Or go slow?

Before you rush into anything, take a moment to think about what growth can mean for your company. In a "use-it-or-lose-it" world, most of us feel compelled to build on our blessings, whether or not we're ready. But growth is, now more than ever, a strategic decision. Just know that whatever route you choose to follow, you can again turn to your network for a range of information, support and resources.

Your business and personal goals will determine whether you quit your day job (about half of all home-based businesses are part-time ventures), enter into strategic partnerships or even slow the growth of your business.

"I decided to slow growth right now because I'm not 100-percent clear on the direction my business should take," admits Laura Gates. Two years ago she launched The Gates Group, a firm specializing in marketing and public relations for woman-owned businesses. After four months, she was turning a profit and well on her way to business "boomlet."

Suddenly, she found herself at a crossroads. The logical avenue for her company seemed to be moving out of her home office into a larger space and hiring employees to handle the extra work. But in promoting her business, Gates discovered she had a talent and enthusiasm for public speaking. She couldn't help wondering where that might lead.

"It's tough," she admits. "I watch my clients growing by leaps and bounds and think, 'I want that.' But I also know how much stress they're under. And I don't know if I want that. I realized I was already starting to neglect my current clients. It's time to get back to basics, which is what got me where I am so far," she says.

In this chapter, you'll meet women whose creative networking styles have matured along with their businesses. Their approaches to growth range from conservative to highly inventive—despite the fact that we women have somehow acquired a reputation for being cautious when it comes to growth.

And just how accurate is that reputation, anyway?

Are you a mouse or a gazelle?

The terminology is telling. Slow-growing companies are classified as "mice" by some analysts. Fast-trackers are "gazelles." Would you rather be characterized a small, shy rodent or a swift and graceful sprinter?

Let's face it. Fast-track companies grab all the glory. And on the surface at least, most of them seem to be run by men. More than 90 percent of the 1994 Inc. 500—*Inc.* magazine's annual list of America's fastest-growing private companies—were owned by men. But it's important to look behind the headlines and determine the real value, relevance and accuracy of statistics. For instance, the *Inc.* superstars are selected from a self-nominating pool, and there's no published record of their performance or position on the list over two or three consecutive years.

The first major study to explore gender differences as a component of business growth was conducted by the National Foundation for Women Business Owners (NFWBO) in 1992. It concluded that women-owned businesses tend to be smaller and report lower annual sales than businesses in the general population. However, the study acknowledged that 20 percent of the woman-owned businesses had been around for fewer than four years.

Recently, a more in-depth study was commissioned by *Biz* magazine. The study concluded that gender alone has little to do with how fast a company will grow. In fact, when companies of similar age and size were compared using traditional markers, 21 percent of the male-owned and 18 percent of the female-owned businesses qualified as high-growth, meaning they had grown an average 20 percent over the past four years.

It appears that women who choose rapid growth tend to achieve it. A 1995 study by Dun & Bradstreet Information Services and NFWBO found that employment in women-owned and operated firms increased by 11.6 percent between 1991 and 1994—more than twice the rate of growth for all U.S. companies during that period!

There are decided benefits to growth. According to the Small Business Administration (SBA), companies with at least 20 employees seem better able to survive economic downturns. Growing bigger can put you in line for tax incentives and in a better position to attract investors and negotiate better terms with suppliers.

But not everyone is comfortable with rapid growth.

Good reasons to stay small

If we women business owners are making different choices than our male counterparts, it may be because we lack financing or need to balance family responsibilities with work. Or it may be that we just feel less pressure to conform to the traditional male model. In fact, about 80 percent of *all* businesses choose to stay small. Technology makes it possible—and often more profitable—for many information-based businesses to keep things scaled down.

And because of this, more of us are looking at the realities of rapid growth and asking, "What's so bad about staying small?"

"If you graph the history of a successful gazelle, you'll see lots of peaks and valleys," says Chris Gibbons, manager of the Office of Business and Industry Affairs in Littleton, Colorado, in an interview in *Home Office Computing Magazine*. Gibbons helps local gazelles take the risks necessary to add jobs and spring into national and international markets.

Successful entrepreneurs know that dynamic growth can really complicate things. When you're focused on pursuing new goals, it becomes more difficult to give customers the level of personal service they've come to expect. Adding too many heads too soon can bury you in paperwork—not to mention extra expenses that may ultimately put you out of business. And investors often trade capital for more control of the business than you're really ready to give.

For these reasons and others, many women are content with stability. Of course, there may come a day when you want to become a gazelle. But for those who don't, there are also a number of ways to add to profitability and take on more challenging work—in other words, become a mightier "mouse."

New sources of information

"How can I tap into export markets?" "What kinds of financing options are available?" "Where can I find a business partner?" If you're suddenly plagued by tough new questions that defy your available resources, rejoice. You're experiencing growing pains.

"If access to strategic information is the problem, and if you're looking for it, you're ready to grow," says Phil Burgess, director of the Center for the New West, a Denver-based economic think tank, in an interview for *Working Woman* magazine's "Is Bigger Better?" section. As you'll see, information can come through a variety of resources.

Contact experts. "I can truly say that some of my best friends are in other cities," says international training specialist Polly Pattison. They are also part of a network she has nurtured over the course of her career. When she discovered she had a knack for teaching design to graphic communicators, Pattison decided the best way to achieve national prominence was to reach out to the people already at the top of the field.

She read their books, attended their seminars, wrote to them and approached them in person. In doing so, she found a generosity of spirit that helped her career and blossomed into friendships and productive business relationships. When she was just getting her feet wet, she approached internationally known designer and trainer Jan White after his workshop at a national conference for magazine publishers.

"He told me he had to catch a train that evening, but said we could have 45 minutes in the cafeteria downstairs," Pattison says. "I asked if I could use some of his ideas in my workshop and he said, 'Of course!' That was the beginning of a lasting friendship. We are in touch every other month or so. We teach together in England."

Sure, introducing yourself to someone with "celebrity" status takes guts. And it's fair to say you won't always be welcomed with open arms. After all, there are status-conscious people in every industry. But if you are courteous and considerate, most people—often the best people—will be genuinely pleased to lend you the benefit of their experience. (Think of it as a way of to ferret out the experts from the egos.)

Learn from your peers. Under pressure to satisfy clients who are focused on creating a presence that is "bigger and better and cooler than the competition," event planners like Donna Wotton, owner of Unconventional Promotions, often find themselves treading in ever more complex technical territory. The more technically ambitious the project, the more her project teams, made up of Wotton's staffers and independent specialists, depend on each other's expertise to pull them out of sticky situations.

"We learn from each other all the time," she says. At one conference, the company hired to build slide presentations was having trouble getting the slides to run smoothly. After trying everything, they still couldn't figure out the source of the problem. At that point, the entire team put their heads together. When the technical support staff suggested a solution, "sure enough, the slides ran lickety-split." Wotton also points out that the solution was an investment in better business. "It changed how the presentation company is going to build presentations from now on. That one tip alone will probably catapult them into a whole new league."

Wotton is quick to add that, in her business, the process of sharing information is active and ongoing. "We meet and exchange so much on the trade show floor," she says. In her regular tours of show floors, she is likely to trade war stories and recommendations and gather important "inside" information. For example, one planner's report on a particular vendor—"We really liked him, but his charges went through the roof!"—is likely to spread like wildfire.

Check out new online resources. Perhaps you're familiar with some of the small-business or home business online forums we mentioned in the previous chapter. Now you need more in-depth information on a specialized area. A growing array of specialized databases and services can put you in touch with potential investors, partners or teachers. A list of possibilities follows:

- **Capital resources.** Business Opportunities Online helps entrepreneurs and investors find each other via eight online databases. By logging onto the Capital Available database, for example, you can gather detailed information on more than 500 investors—from private lenders to venture capital firms—with a few thousand dollars up to $25 million to spare. Each profile contains detailed information about the investor's lending patterns and industry preferences.

- **Training.** If you need help creating a sales brochure and pricing your products, you can consult Entrepreneurial Edge Online. From the comfort of your home office, you can learn from one of 120 online tutorials offered.

- **Partners.** As you grow, taking on a partner with complementary skills or resources you lack can be a savvy move. Among the 13 small-business categories available on Entrepreneurs Online is a business leads section that matches businesses with professionals willing to work for a mix of salary plus equity.

- **New markets.** With access to the International Trade Network, you can research export services, scout for leads abroad and advertise your business to worldwide subscribers free via e-mail.

Create an advisory board. If you've been operating a home-based business, you'll probably agree that isolation makes a less than perfect business partner. You may find yourself wondering, "Is this idea sound, or just a good beginning?" Even one other person can make a difference, by providing a different point of view, challenging your thinking or helping you brainstorm ways to flesh out promising ideas and strategies.

When Susan Petes invited a dozen of her clients to act as a formal board of advisers for her training company, she was prepared to sweeten the deal by offering each new member a free training session. As it turned out, her clients needed no incentive to participate. The group meets regularly to critique aspects of her company operations and offer solutions to prickly problems. "More than anything else, the meetings are a reality check," she reported in *Inc.* magazine. While discussions can be "brutally candid," the input from members, who represent the wide variety of her clients, is invaluable.

Susan RoAne, author of *How to Work a Room* and *The Secrets of Savvy Networking*, started a different type of group composed of self-employed professionals. "I started off by asking my accountant, my stockbroker and my attorney to dinner," she writes. Although each member comes from a different field, the group finds that many of the topics discussed, such as business management and financing, affect everyone. According to RoAne, each member's goal should be to help other members. "It's an environment in which business issues can be discussed without the threat of criticism."

If you're thinking about establishing an advisory group, bravo! Here are a few ground rules.

- **Determine the purpose of the group.** Do you want feedback from the people you sell to, or support and information that will bolster your business? In the first case, you will follow Petes' example and go directly to your customers. Otherwise you're better off selecting other business professionals with expertise in areas you know you're weak in.
- **Choose the right people.** If you plan to target customers, select people who accurately represent the demographics of your customer base. If you're targeting other business professionals, ask people with acknowledged expertise in areas you need to know more about.

- **Determine the commitment you expect.** Do you plan to meet regularly? Will meetings be formal "focus" groups or informal gab sessions? Let prospective board members know what kind of information you want to gather. Do you want input that will lead to product improvements or feedback on how a current marketing campaign is being received? Who will lead meetings? When, if ever, will the group disband or accept new members?

  If you're putting together a customer advisory board, it's wise to turn the reins over to someone else. If you're meeting with other business professionals, you might share leadership.

- **Be sure to offer a reward or incentive.** After all, you are asking people for time and energy. You may offer customers a free product or substantial discount on your services. Or you may decide on a good dinner before every meeting. If customer-representatives decline your offer, plan to give them a commemorative pen or plaque at the end of their service.

  If you're meeting to pick the brains of other business professionals, focus on mutual support. This is not a way to get your taxes done free, it's an information exchange. Don't let things get out of balance.

- Keep things confidential. Enough said.

Change your affiliations to match your changing needs. The problems of someone at the senior level are different than people just starting up. The more expertise you gain, the fewer ideas you're likely to get at broad industry events.

For example, the computer industry's love affair with ever-bigger and better national conferences and trade show has propelled Donna Wotton's event-planning business into the stratosphere. The problems she now shares with 100 or so of nation's top event planners are best addressed at meetings of the Computer Exhibit Managers Association (CEMA) rather than generalized networking functions for the event-planning business.

New sources of support

Of course, you still need ongoing emotional support. But you may also need help handling the overflow of work or a financial shot in the arm. If you're home-based, hiring your first employee can mean running up against zoning laws. No matter what your business plans, you won't make a go of it without business partners, strategic alliances and other support resources.

Partner with vendors. There are a number of ways that partnering with vendors can help your business grow. Some provide solutions to short-term projects or cash flow crunches. Some set the stage for long-term, mutually beneficial business alliances.

- **Financing.** If you resell inventory or sell goods that you manufacture, your suppliers may agree to ship you the necessary materials and give you 60 to 90 days to pay for them—allowing you to collect from your customers. A jewelry designer might float $1,000 to $5,000 this way. Of course, most suppliers will not offer rock-bottom prices for goods under this arrangement. But over the short-term, it can help you preserve your cash flow.

- **Resources.** Wotton's event-planning business depends on what she calls a "resource exchange." She identifies the best talent for her short-term project teams based on recommendations she gets from other event planners. For Wotton and other senior event planners, relationships with ad hoc team members are long-term investments.

  When a colleague she'd depended on to provide technical support for computer events lost one of his major customers, Wotton and two other event planners stepped forward and committed a year's worth of business to him. Now he supports about 20 different event planners. "Of course, when a client asks him who he'd recommend to coordinate a particular event one of us is suited for, he recommends us," Wotton says. "And the network comes back this way again."

- **Distribution.** Ruth Owades, founder and president of Calyx & Corolla, a company that provides overnight delivery of fresh-cut flowers, used technology to "marry" her company with a diverse group of vendors. "We don't have everyone under one roof, but resources like our growers and FedEx act as if they are part of our company," she explained in *Working Woman* magazine.

  To streamline the process of distributing the flowers, Owades plugs each of her vendors into Calyx & Corolla's state-of-the-art computer system. As soon as an order is received, it appears on computer screens at local growers' offices as well as at Federal Express. The cooperative aspect is: All the vendors have the opportunity to benefit from more business.

Knowing that it would take much more than the appropriate technology to make this cooperative distribution system work, Owades took time and care to personally introduce the concept to each vendor, especially local growers, many of whom had never touched a computer before.

Partner with a mentor. "Last year, I got frustrated trying to figure out how to expand with no money," says Nancy Kingscott. When she started Nancy K. & Co. six years earlier, she was selling holiday breakfast breads she baked in a friend's oven while holding down a full-time job at I. Magnin. Soon, she was doing a booming business at the local farmer's market. She had also developed a brisk wholesale trade with local delicatessens. But when a classmate in a commercial baking class suggested she add a cinnamon-sugar cookie called a snickerdoodle to her repertoire, her sales really took off.

Over the years, Kingscott had grown accustomed to blazing her own trail and learning what she needed to know as she went along. But after enrolling in the Women's Initiative for Self-Employment (WISE) business planning courses and participating in regular Food Action Groups, she felt the time was right to bring in some outside expertise.

Because she felt marketing was a weak link in her plan to grow her business, she requested a WISE mentor with experience in that area. Together Nancy and her mentor developed a series of promotional postcards with clever teaser messages to promote her baked goods. It was a strategy that had gotten results for her mentor.

The WISE mentor program pairs successful women business owners with women, like Kingscott, who have been in business at least one year and are ready to expand. Mentors and protégés are paired according the goal of the protégé. In the process of taking specific steps toward that goal over a six-month period, the duo might talk on the phone, meet at a cafe or visit each others' offices.

"Everybody works differently," say program administrator Tomoko Lipp. "The only thing we ask of each mentor is to give four hours a month. That's the minimum. A lot of people give much more than that." In the process, she says, it is common for duos to bond and opt to continue the relationship on an informal level.

The close, confidential nature of the mentor/protégé relationship encourages protégés to let their guards down and share uncertainties they might not be so inclined to admit to a colleague. Mentors provide information, feedback, support and coaching. In the process, insights can pop up spontaneously.

"You get tunnel vision sometimes," says Kingscott. "Many little improvements can be made when somebody else starts really looking at what you're doing."

New sources of exposure

Now that your business is on its feet, you may want to expand your client base, build new distribution channels or reach into international markets. Here are some strategies for increasing the visibility of your business as you grow.

Move into an executive suite. You're too big for your home office and too robust for a business incubator, but not yet ready for a real commitment to leased office space. Or maybe you need regular access to specific types of facilities, such as a conference room, or to business services, such as typing.

Executive suites may provide an answer. These office-in-a-box set-ups are located in urban high-rises as well as suburban office parks. They offer big company comforts at a pay-as-you-go price, typically on a month-to-month basis. While you'll pay more than you would for comparable office space, you're not obligated to commit yourself to a long-term lease.

And like incubators, executive suites offer excellent opportunities to network with other tenants.

Take on a leadership role. Sandy Sohcot had built a steady clientele as a business consultant. After her husband died, she decided to slow the growth for a couple of years to regroup. When she was ready to move ahead with her business, one of her priorities was to establish a reputation outside of her existing sphere of influence.

"I had a referral base from a very close group of people, but I really wasn't known outside of that group," she says. After trying the formal leads group through the chamber of commerce and creating her informal group, she landed at National Association for Women Business Owners (NAWBO).

She quickly became involved, planning programs, such as town meetings and open houses, and teaming up with other members to conduct skill-building exchanges. "It was an opportunity to show who I was and get to know other members."

Sandy gained even greater visibility when she stepped up to help the chapter president organize the budgeting process for her new board. All her hard work led to a nomination she accepted—to serve as president of the chapter.

"There is no question that it is a benefit to me professionally, as well as helping me to learn and develop new skills," Sohcot says. "My philosophy is do something you enjoy and really want to do, and trust that the business will follow."

Set up shop on the World Wide Web. For as little as a $1,000 initial fee, plus an additional $100 a month to gain access through a service provider, you can launch your business into cyberspace via the World Wide Web.

Before you jump on the bandwagon, know that this is not a venue to every business. For example, if your market is largely women who stay at home with their families, you will not finding many of your potential customers cruising the Internet...yet.

If you do decide your business is ripe for an international venue like cyberspace, you will have to invest time in planning a clever way to present your products and services—and then continually update the information to lure browsers back repeatedly. Admittedly, competing against companies with deep pockets can set you back a bit. Your best bet is to focus on—you guessed it—building relationships with your potential customers through two-way communication. Allow them to provide feedback and input and respond in a timely fashion.

New sources of referrals

No matter what your growth strategy, it's always wise to review your networking activity to see if you're really giving and getting all that you can from it. As your business grows, you'll need to be more creative in your search for referrals. Here are a few ideas to get your creative juices flowing:

Go after those gatekeepers. Amy Jussell, an award-winning copywriter, deals with gatekeepers—you know, those people whose sole purpose seems to be to protect their bosses from any communication from the outside world—all the time. "The gymnastics required with many (advertising) agencies these days is becoming an Olympic event," she wrote in *Me!dea* magazine. "No longer do you hear 'Can you talk to so-and-so now?' because they don't even ask. If you're unknown to the firm, you'll be asked by an overloaded staffer in creative services, 'So, what do you do?' Then, you have approximately six seconds to respond, eight if you're award-winning. Usually this is followed by 'We don't need anybody right now.' Of course, when they need you they really, really need you."

You may not have considered gatekeepers as part of your network. But if gatekeepers have the power to bar you from delivering your message to the people you want in your network, then doesn't the gatekeeper need to belong as well?

Make an effort to learn the first name of each gatekeeper you encounter. Then, treat her like she's the most important person in the company. (You're not being phony. At this point, she *is* the most important person to you.) You might say, "Donna, I can see how busy you are this afternoon, but I'd really love to work with Primo Agency. Do you mind if I call you in a month or so, just in case you might have an opening for someone with my abilities?"

When you do call, ask for Donna and take a moment to chat and perhaps commiserate over the feast-and-famine life of advertising. If you are *sincerely* polite, as well as persistent, Donna (who is as human as the rest of us) is more likely to remember you when something does come up.

Share your new goals. Maybe you're planning to diversify or change the direction of your business. When you're talking with networking contacts, say so. Don't fish for referrals. Instead, make your approach open-ended. Ask for feedback, information and resources in a no-pressure way that will encourage your network contacts to give some thought to how they might be of help, or who they can refer you to.

When Betsy Brill decided to begin focusing more on writing and editing and targeting new industries, she turned back to familiar Woman in Communications, Inc. (WICI) connections. Her investment paid off. At a gathering of friends, Brill told a woman she hadn't seen for a while about the career shift she was planning to make. Her friend said, "If you're interested in medical writing, I could really keep you busy."

Soon after the gathering, Brill's samples were in the mail. "Even though she had seen things that I'd written over the years, I wanted her to see the professional things I'd done (outside WICI). I've been working for her regularly now. You have to remember to talk to people about what you're doing," she says.

Develop a niche. In the beginning, being all things to all people may be a fine way to survive. But now that you've established yourself, maybe it's time to developing a specialty that will set you apart from the competition.

Communicating a narrower specialty to your network contacts will help them remember what you do. As you become known for providing a particular type of service, potential customers will have a built-in reason to seek you out. If you're not sure what niche might be most lucrative, begin by polling network contacts who might be prospective customers. Is there a need that's not being filled, or filled well, by the people you compete with?

Teach. When Polly Pattison left her job as art director for Up With People to start her design business, she had no intention of training her clients.

But that's what they were clamoring for. After conducting informal workshops locally, she thought she might be on to something. She contacted the International Association of Business Communicators (IABC) and began doing workshops for the local membership.

"That was my first experience with formal training," Pattison says. She conducted her first three workshops on her home turf in Southern California before "brazenly" presenting a proposal to officials of the organization at its national headquarters in San Francisco. Once again, it worked.

This endorsement, in turn, brought her national—and ultimately international—exposure when an organization called Dynamic Graphics Educational Foundation added her course to their training roster. "It has given me credibility and some spin-off business," Pattison says.

Expand your 'contact sphere.' Networking author Ivan Misner suggests identifying a group of complementary businesses and professions that can provide you with a steady source of leads. "For example, if you put a lawyer, CPA, financial planner and banker in same room, you couldn't *stop* them from doing business," he says.

Who could you include in your contact sphere? A graphic designer might target printers, writers, service bureaus and marketing consultants. A carpenter might focus on painters, plumbers, landscapers and electricians. A wedding photographer could work with caterers, travel agents and florists.

Advertise your expertise. Speaking before groups, writing books and articles, conducting workshops and granting interviews are all effective ways to establish expertise with potential customers and build your referral network. Nonprofit organizations and continuing education courses are always searching for qualified speakers willing to donate their time and expertise—even if they're unpracticed.

Conclusion

At every stage of business development, networking is a vital component of success. You may choose to grow your business and enter the corporate world on your own terms (as your own corporation) or you may choose to keep it small. But no matter what choice you make, networking will support it.

We've looked at the many ways networking can support your business endeavors. But from the beginning of this book, we've emphasized that successful networking requires you to *give* something. In the next chapter, we'll look at ways you can give to women in the world of business who could benefit from your expertise and to the causes and organizations you believe in.

Chapter 17

Making a difference, making way

"Success and achievement mean nothing if you don't bring somebody else along. Because, when it's all said and done, it's not going to matter what your billings were or how many awards you won or what kind of car you drove. It will be about how many peoples' lives you lit up and how many people you lifted as you climbed."

There was a profound silence, then long, thunderous applause for Terrie Williams at the close of her address at the San Francisco Women In Communications, Inc. (WICI) chapter's "Leading Change Awards."

Williams started her public relations agency with no money, clients or business credentials. Today The Terrie Williams Agency represents some of the country's top corporations, as well as entertainment and sports figures. The secrets of her success include simple acts of consideration, such as treating everyone she meets with courtesy and respect. These have also been the building blocks that have provided a means for Williams to give something back.

We've come a long way. A dozen years ago, women were trying to live by the rules of a man's world. We were afraid to be too courteous when we should have been calculating. The managers we worked for were constantly looking over our shoulders, and often leery of extending a hand. It didn't make much sense, but it was the only game in town.

Not so anymore. Somewhere along the line we discovered our power and realized we don't have to play by the old rules any longer. Instead, we've invented a few of our own, by doing what comes naturally—working with and for each other.

Womankind: finding ways to share the wealth

In the space of a single generation, there has been a wild swing in female archetypes, from Donna Reed to Superwoman. And during that time, women have learned a few things about what's practical...and what's possible.

Today, we don't have to separate our professional selves from our personal values. Women have developed confidence and clout, and we've discovered it's quite possible to integrate good business with good work that can lead to change at the individual, social or political level. And once again, networking can support this agenda.

Today, women have more expertise, time and money to give. Some choose to act individually by providing a supportive wing for younger or less experienced protégés. Some use their businesses, companies or organizations as vehicles for making their community or the world a better place to live.

In this chapter, we look at women, as well as the organizations they belong to, who are choosing to make a difference. They demonstrate that courage and personal convictions have a place in the networking process. Here are some examples of how women are getting involved, and networking to make a difference:

Paving the way for political progress. Although women represent more than half the U.S. population, in 1995 a whopping 92 percent of Congressional representatives were male. Geraldine Ferraro reminded participants of a National Association for Female Executives' (NAFE) Satellite Conference of this lopsided statistic, noting that the figure stood at 98 percent the year before.

Progress in representation is the priority of EMILY's list. EMILY is an acronym for "Early Money Is Like Yeast" (in other words, it makes the "dough" rise). EMILY's list is a Democratic women's network representing 34,000 members across the nation that, to date, has raised more money for political candidates than any other political action committee.

Despite the fact that more women are in a position to work from the inside out—nudging new legislation through state governments, for example—budget cuts in a New Congress are a signal that we remain vulnerable.

Networking has made us resourceful, however. When the 18-year-old women's congressional bipartisan caucus lost its funding, some member-Congresswomen had no qualms about working outside the system. They formed a nonprofit research association called Women's Policy, Inc., to raise money from corporations and foundations in support of the issues they sponsor.

Making headway on issues such as pay equity can be difficult on an individual level, employee to manager. But with the grass roots support of members, women's professional organizations can press for pay equity within a certain industry or nationwide and even demand accountability.

As part of an all-out campaign to get every member of Congress to support key women's issues, NAFE recently published "7 Principles of Workplace Equity" in its *Executive Female* magazine. Number one on the list: "Women and men should be judged by work performance alone and compensated accordingly."

NAFE has made it easy for even its busiest members to get involved by providing a form letter readers can sign and forward directly to representatives in Congress. NAFE plans to publish the names of representatives who sign on to supporting the seven principles.

Creating networking groups. Her isolation as a home-based business owner prompted Thérèse Watley to wonder if there were others like herself who were interested in getting together to exchange ideas, resources and experiences. She wasn't surprised to attract both veterans and new start-ups with her initial mailing. Only after she'd brought everyone together in the Home-based Entrepreneur Network (HEN) did she realize, "I'm the only one running my business full-time!"

Before long, she found herself preaching the gospel of making the break. "I understand that it's very scary, especially if you're making $60,000 or $70,000 a year. But if you remove that outside stress, you can work that much harder at your business, and make that much more money."

When members of NAFE, her group's umbrella organization, started calling from around the country, Watley began using online forums to track the groundswell of new home-business entrepreneurs. She found a growing group in need of information, support and, in many cases, the confidence to fly solo. She is so committed to spreading the word that she plans to take the group to a national level.

"I'm compelled to help women develop the confidence and skills they need to become more successful in their own businesses." She plans to parlay her own expertise as a public relations and marketing consultant into creating a full-fledged media campaign.

Frustrated by what she calls a "very, very severe glass ceiling" that bars many women from sitting on the board of her professional organization, Gretchen Minney took the initiative to found an informal women's networking group.

Because the majority of member bookstores in the National Association of College Stores (NACS) are small, the majority of managers tend to be women. "These women give endless hours of time to committees," Minney, director of the Auraria Book Center in Denver, says. "Then, when it comes time to select board members, the (typically majority-male) board will draft another man." Minney's aim was to encourage women to talk about shared experiences and learn more about how to work within the system.

Reaching out to other entrepreneurs. Like many other home-based entrepreneurs, Jill and Al Svoboda often felt isolated and had difficulty finding advice and information geared to local home-based companies. So they created their own resource.

Today, the Svobodas' *Home and Small Business Reporter* is a 32-page tabloid-style magazine picked up by as many as 22,000 interested readers at 300 locations throughout the Chicago area. Advertising revenues support the free publication, although the Svobodas try to keep rates low for merchants who want to promote their services and products.

In addition to feature articles on everything from financing to how preserve your marriage while operating a home-based business, there is a calendar of local small-business meetings, events and seminars, which provide ongoing opportunities for local networking.

Giving away expertise. A successful business consultant, Tomoko Lipp, finds it rewarding to help women who would otherwise be unable to afford her services reach their business goals. Working part-time for the Women's Initiative for Self-Employment (WISE), she teaches business courses, conducts specialized industry "action groups" and oversees the mentorship program.

"Most of my (regular) clients are men, and very few are young," Lipp says. "The interesting thing about working with women is that they open up and tell me about their personal goals—what success means to them."

Through WISE, Lipp is able to work with a more diverse "clientele"— many facing ethnic barriers she struggled to break through. "Because I am of Japanese descent, I understand cultural gaps," she says. "I think women are finding now how much power women have working together. It's really a wonderful feeling to be part of it."

Becoming a mentor. When Kathleen O'Brien joined Montgomery, McCracken, Walker & Rhoads, there were two other women working for the Philadelphia law firm. Thanks to her recruiting and mentoring efforts, profiled in *Working Woman* magazine, more than a third of the 150 lawyers are women. "Now we have a history of being mentors to one another and helping young associates. What we give them is a safe information channel, a reality check of sorts, on how they're being perceived, who they should be trying to work with and what kinds of cases they should be working on," she says.

While some of the most effective mentoring relationships are conducted on an informal basis, many women are starting structured programs in their companies. Catalyst, a research organization for women, has helped women at dozens of companies develop proposals, and publishes a 65-page guide to mentoring.

Mentoring programs have also proven to give new employees a better beginning at some companies. Every employee who starts work at Great Plains Software in Fargo, North Dakota, enters a three-month program. In addition to attending eight formal classes covering company policies and procedures, each new hire is paired with a senior person who serves as coach. At the end of the orientation, managers use feedback from the "coaches" as well as from orientation classmates to help new employees get started on the right foot.

Southwest Airlines also pairs new hires with senior people through a quasi-mentoring program called "Co-Hearts." The idea is to give a new person someone to bounce ideas off of as well as an immediate friend in the company.

You may feel more comfortable mentoring women outside your company. Some universities and colleges have mentoring programs in which students correspond with and job-shadow alumni for an inside view of company life that can help them choose a career. Mentors have even hired protégés for summer internships. (Check with the alumni office of your college or university about the availability of such programs or the possibility of pioneering a new one.) Other potential protégés might include gifted students who need help choosing a college or economically disadvantaged girls.

Teaching the next generation. "I started hiring and placing interns pretty early on in my business," says event planner Donna Wotton. When one intern she had hired full-time was wooed by an offer she couldn't match, Wotton reluctantly let her go. A mentor, like a parent, can't hold on too tight. "She went with my blessing," Wotton says. "We both felt working inside a company was an important part of her career development."

Even after the relationship moved to this new level, Wotton followed through, using her experience to coach her protégé into corporate America. "Whenever she has a political situation she doesn't know how to deal with, she calls me up and we talk it through."

But increasingly the relationship is maturing. "She doesn't think that she's my peer, she still has me somewhere up on a pedestal," Wotton says. "But I see her as a senior-level peer now. She's terribly flattered if I call her up and say 'I'm stumped on this one. I need somebody to bounce some ideas off of.' So she's become a real resource for me as well."

Raising consciousness. When she moved from Oakland, California, to Fairfield, Iowa, so that her husband could pursue his doctorate, Marilyn Johnson Kondwani found herself in a very different world. "I'm an African-American woman and I live in a town where there are no other African-Americans. But we have our Midwestern upbringing in common."

It was enough of bond for the wife, mother, businesswoman and graduate student to form the Self-Esteem Dream Team. The goal of the organization is to inspire and encourage women to achieve their dreams, whatever they might be. "In this area of the country, men are wary of their wives spending $25 to join a woman's group," Kondwani laughs. "They think 'something's going to happen, and my dinner's not gonna be on the table.' "

Through her efforts and example, she hopes to promote the value of diversity and self-esteem by making small inroads in her rural community.

Forming an investment club. As women have accumulated wealth, most admit their investment acumen has not followed suit. Rather than tough it out on their own, more women are joining investment clubs to build college funds and retirement savings as they learn the ins and outs of investing.

Popularized by the Beardstown Business and Professional Women's Investment Club of Beardstown, Illinois, which has boasted an annual return of 23.4 percent over the last 10 years, investment clubs tend to perform as well as or better than the stock market, according to the National Association of Investors Corporation (NAIC). Once again, the team concept seems to turn to gold for women. All-female clubs slightly outperform all-male clubs, with lifetime earning rates of 10.5 percent versus 9.7 percent.

Members (who should share a long-term outlook) typically meet once a month to pool monthly dues and share the burden of researching companies and tracking stock performance. Clubs are legal entities that must conform to certain regulations. NAIC advises its 13,000 member investment clubs about a range of issues.

Dressing others for success. How do you dress for success when you can't afford the clothes? Low-income women as well as women who are rejoining the work force after a long absence face this barrier that often leads to low self-esteem.

This prompted Charlotte Krumwiede to found Career Closet in 1992. Since then, the San Jose, California, organization has dressed about 1,600 job applicants—most of whom receive public assistance and are enrolled in job training programs—in designer suits and dresses, as well as matching shoes and accessories. All the clothing is donated. There are similar nonprofit groups in Chicago, New York City, Miami and Washington, D.C.

Giving encouragement to the next generation. Despite progress in some fields such as medicine, science remains an overwhelmingly male domain. In fact, *Science Magazine* has even devoted several special issues to women in science, addressing the overt discrimination that often discourages young girls from entering the field. This has prompted women professionals to find ways to reach out and share their experience with young women and girls.

In 1994, 50 of the nation's top female scientists gathered at Mills College in Oakland, California, for a two-day "Women in Science Summit." Their goal was to examine the obstacles girls and women face and develop a practical agenda to encourage women to go into science.

Coming full circle

Of course, there are many ways to make a difference through business, and some of them are not so exclusively dependent upon networking relationships as those we've just considered. For instance, companies like Ben & Jerry's and The Body Shop have proven that it's possible to create a bond with your customers based on shared values. Hanna Anderson, the $44 million mail-order company from Portland, Oregon, has shown us how a business can have a "heart" through their "Hannadowns" program, which offers customers credit for returning used Hanna Anderson children's clothing. The company then donates the durable, cotton clothing to needy children.

These companies and many more like them are integrating a sense of social responsibility with day-to-day operations. You may choose to do the same with your business, or opt to work directly with others, passing along the information, support and referrals you have to offer. Either way, you'll be rewarded in helping others.

And that's what networking is all about. Remember our definition: The ongoing process of building and maintaining personal and professional relationships through reciprocal communication and sharing of information with individuals and groups of individuals.

"Wherever you are in life, if you give something to someone, you'll make a difference," Terrie Williams said in her speech. And through the give-and-take that is networking, almost anything is possible.

Conclusion

Reading the daily field reports from the United Nations Fourth World Conference on Women (going on in China, as this book goes to press), we were astounded by the magnitude of this networking event. An estimated 36,000 women—many of them working women—have made this the largest grass roots gathering of our gender ever held. Although the specifics of their individual lives probably vary widely from Peru to Peoria, these women also share many of the same problems. Collectively, they will lobby for policy changes on issues running the gamut from health care to wages.

It's likely that more than a few promises made by member governments will go unfulfilled at the close of this conference (although the official Grass Roots Organization means to keep score!). But who can accurately gauge how many meaningful personal connections will be made there? How many solutions shared? That is an *immediate* legacy.

Many of us will never take part in networking on such a grand scale. But who's to say that the daily interactions of "ordinary" women are anything short of extraordinary? We hope the Fourth World Conference will change the world through the collective networking efforts of women. But in the meantime it is shining a light on the potential of each individual to enhance even one life—as a mentor, a sounding board or a resource. There is also magnitude in that.

Resources and organizations

Women's professional organizations

National Association of Women Business Owners
1100 Wayne Ave., Suite 830
Silver Springs, MD 20910
301-608-2590
Fax: 301-608-2596

Workshops, seminars, referral services, active local groups and local and national meetings and events. NAWBO keeps members informed through monthly and quarterly communications and a membership directory. Its research arm, the National Foundation of Women in Business, studies women in business. Annual national dues are $75, with a one-time registration fee of $25.

American Women's Economic Development Corporation
71 Vanderbilt Ave., 3rd Fl.
New York, NY 10169
800-222-AWED

National organization with 2,000 members. Offers a hotline and one-on-one consultation with experts in every area of small business. Advice and workshops for women business owners. Annual membership fee is $55.

American Business Women's Association
9100 Ward Parkway
Box 8728
Kansas City, MO 64114
816-361-6621

National organization with 90,000 members and 1,800 local groups provides opportunities for women to help themselves and others grow personally and professionally through leadership, education, networking support, national recognition, resume service, loan programs, national and regional meetings. Annual dues for national membership are $45 for the first year, $30 thereafter. Local chapters may charge additional dues.

National Association for Women in Education
1325 18th St. NW, Suite 210
Washington, DC 20036-6511
202-659-9330

NAWE serves women in administration, counseling, activities and services, instruction and research—in higher education and in institutions and agencies related to higher education. It offers members opportunities to affiliate with subnetworks to seek out women with similar interests, find a mentor, identify colleagues who share similar interests and concerns. Members receive a quarterly journal and quarterly newsletters. Research awards program, women's issues projects and annual conferences. Membership is $65 a year.

National Association for Female Executives
30 Irving Pl., 5th Fl.
New York, NY 10003
800-927-6233
212-477-2200

With more than 250,000 members, NAFE is the largest businesswomen's organization in the country, dedicated to the advancement of women in the workplace through education and networking. It hosts career conferences and seminars, sponsors a career data bank, publishes a resume guide and offers a writing service. In addition, there are resource sharing groups, educational programs, a speakers bureau, a membership directory and a bimonthly magazine. There are more than 200 local affiliates. The annual fee is $29.

American Society of Women Accountants (ASWA)
1255 Lynnfield Rd., Suite 257
Memphis, TN 38119
800-326-2163
901-680-0470

Nearly 6,500 ASWA members participate in 110 local chapters nationwide. And the group is open to accountants, bookkeepers or individuals—women and men—interested in accounting. Local activities are primarily for networking opportunities, but the organization also offers programs that qualify for CPE credit, scholarship programs and other events. National membership dues are $75, with additional fees for local affiliation.

American Women in Radio & Television
1101 Connecticut Ave. NW, Suite 700
Washington, DC 20036
202-429-5102

Its goal is to advance the impact of women in the electronic media and allied fields by educating, advocating and acting as a resource to its members and the industry. Monthly meetings are held by local chapters, which offer networking opportunities, panel discussions and motivational speakers. Annual dues are $125.

National Association of Women in Construction
327 S. Adams St.
Ft. Worth, TX 76104
800-552-3506
817-877-5551

This association is composed of 238 local groups that unite for the mutual benefit of women who are actively employed in the construction industry. The organization provides educational opportunities, scholarships, workshops and annual meetings. Local groups meet on a monthly basis. National dues are $80 annually.

National Federation of Business and Professional Women of the United States of America (BPW/USA)
2012 Massachusetts Ave., NW
Washington, DC 20036
202-293-1100

BPW/USA promotes equity for all women in the workplace through advocacy education and information. There are more than 80,000 members in 2,800 local organizations. BPW/USA has been a leader in passing much of the nation's landmark civil and women's rights legislation including the Child Care Act of 1991. Its foundation conducts research on issues affecting women in the workplace and awards scholarships, loans and grants to women. Annual dues are $50.

National Association of Insurance Women
P.O. Box 4410
Tulsa, OK 74159-5193
800-766-NAIW
918-744-5195
Fax: 918-743-1968

NAIW is dedicated to the professional advancement of its members through educational programs and networking opportunities. Its 500 local, state and regional associations serve 15,000 women and men employed in the risk or insurance field throughout the U.S., Canada and Puerto Rico. Annual dues are approximately $60.

Women in Communications, Inc.
10605 Judicial Dr., Suite A-4
Fairfax, VA 22030
703-359-9000

WICI has more than 10,000 members, men and women, and hundreds of local chapters nationwide. WICI chapters offer regular professional development meetings, job hotlines and annual seminars. National membership, a subscription to the organization's publication, access to a national toll-free jot hotline and professional development opportunities. National dues are $90 a year; local chapter dues vary, but range from $15 to $25 annually.

Other professional organizations

Following is a mere sample of the types of national organizations that offer local affiliations. For a more comprehensive listing, check your library's reference section for the three-volume *Encyclopedia of Associations,* for listings for everything from the Dude Rancher's Association to the National Association of Pizza Operators.

**Computer & Communications
  Industry Association**
666 11th St. NW
Washington, DC 20001
202-783-0070

**American Business Management
  Association**
Box 111
West Hyannis Port, MA 02672
508-790-4567

**American Entrepreneurs
  Association**
2392 Morse Ave.
Irvine, CA 92714
714-261-2325

Direct Marketing Association
11 W. 42nd St.
New York, NY 10036
212-768-7277

**National Association of
  Entrepreneurs**
1400 W. 64th Ave.
Denver, CO 80221
303-426-1166

**National Association of
  Home-Based Businesses**
P.O. Box 30220
Baltimore, MD 21270
410-363-3698

**International Association of
  Business Communicators**
1 Hallidie Plaza, Suite 600
San Francisco, CA 94102
415-433-3400

**American Society for Training
  and Development**
1640 King St.
Alexandria, VA 22313
703-683-8100

**Professional Secretaries
  International**
P.O. Box 20404
Kansas City, MO 64195-0404
816-891-6600
Fax: 816-891-9118

Toastmasters International
23182 Arroyo Vista
Rancho Santa Margarita, Ca 92688
714-858-8255

Service organizations

Kiwanis International
3636 Woodview Trace
Indianapolis, IN 46268
1-800-KIWANIS
317-875-8755

Kiwanis promotional materials suggest that the "opportunity to expand business and professional networking" is one of the its key membership benefits. There are more than 9,000 clubs and nearly 300,000 members worldwide. Kiwanis first permitted women to join in 1987. Today, nearly 45,000 of its members are female. Service emphasis is on young children—through community projects. Most groups meet weekly. The initial fee to join is $15, and members pay approximately $16 every six months.

Lions Club
300 22nd Street
Oak Brook, IL 60521
708-571-5466

With a worldwide membership of 1.4 million, women make up 87,000. Lions clubs are recognized for their service to the blind and visually impaired. An initial entrance fee is $20, and annual dues thereafter is $18. While Lions Club literature doesn't actively promote the networking benefits of membership, it does promote that it creates "meaningful leisure time for you by filling it with fellowship." Most groups meet at least twice a month.

Optimists International
4494 Lindell Boulevard
St. Louis, MO 63108
314-371-6000

Optimists offers "new social and working relationships with individuals from a cross section of our communities and the opportunity to develop and demonstrate leadership skills." There are nearly 4,300 clubs in the U.S. and Canada, and more than 155,000 male and female members. The club's over-riding motto is "A friend of youth." Membership is open to anyone in good standing in the community. Local clubs are run autonomously, so meeting structure and dues vary. Most groups meet weekly or monthly. There is usually a joining fee of $25 or $30. Annual dues range between $40 and $50.

Rotary International
One Rotary Center
1560 Sherman Avenue
Evanston, IL 60201
708-866-3000

"Service above self" is Rotary's motto, although it does concede that membership is an opportunity to build lifelong friendships. There are more than 27,000 Rotary clubs and 1.2 million members worldwide, with 50,000 female members. Membership is by invitation to individuals who hold professional, proprietary, executive or managerial positions. In each club, membership is limited to one representative per occupation, based on a "classification" system. Rotarians carry out a variety of humanitarian endeavors, sponsor scholarships, offer vocational training and more. Clubs meet weekly.

Leads organizations

Business Network Intl.
268 S. Bucknell Avenue
Claremont, CA 91711-4907
800-825-8286
800-624-2227 (in Southern California)

Leads Club
P.O. Box 279
Carlsbad, CA 92018-0279
619-434-3761
800-783-3761

Electronic networking

Job search services

kiNexus
Information Kinetics, Inc.
640 N. LaSalle St.
Suite 560
Chicago, IL 60610
800-229-6499
Fax: 312-642-0616

Job Bank USA
1420 Spring Hill Road
Suite 480
McLean, VA 22102
800-296-1USA
Fax: 703-847-1494

Connexion
Peterson's Connexion Services
202 Carnegie Center
P.O. Box 2123
Princeton, NJ 08543-2123
800-338-3282, ext. 561
Fax: 609-243-9150

Commercial online services

Women's Wire
1820 Gateway Dr.
San Mateo, CA 94404
415-378-6500

America Online (AOL)
869 Westwood Center Dr.
Vienna, VA 22182
800-827-636
Fax: 703-883-1509

CompuServe
500 Arlington Centre Blvd.
P.O. Box 20212
Columbus, OH 43220
800-848-8199

PRODIGY
445 Hamilton Ave.
White Plains, NY 10601
800-PRODIGY
914-993-8000

Other resources

National Business Incubation Association
20 E. Circle Drive
Athens, OH 45701
614-593-4331

The NBIA provides information and professional development activities that help business incubator developers and managers create and administer effective incubation programs. It conducts research and referral services, compiles statistics and maintains a speaker's bureau.

Small Business Administration
409 Third St. SW
Washington, DC 20416
800-827-5722

Call for a recorded message on available resources and programs, such as SCORE and SBDCs.

Mentoring programs

One to One
375 Park Ave., Suite 1705
New York, NY 10152
212-339-0141

One to One is a support organization for mentoring programs that keeps rosters of mentoring organizations in Atlanta, Boston, California, Detroit, Newark and New York.

Catalyst
250 Park Avenue South
New York, NY 10003
212-777-8900

Write for a 65-page guide to mentoring ($45) from this women's research organization.

Executive suites

Alliance Business Centers
18333 Preston Road, Suite 188
Dallas, TX 75252
800-869-9595

HQ Business Centers
20 Montgomery St., Suite 2350
San Francisco, CA 94104
800-480-2020

Index

Cressman Library
Cedar Crest College
Allentown, Pa. 18104

DEMCO